3.00

CLASSIC
TOURING ROUTES
IN SCOTLAND

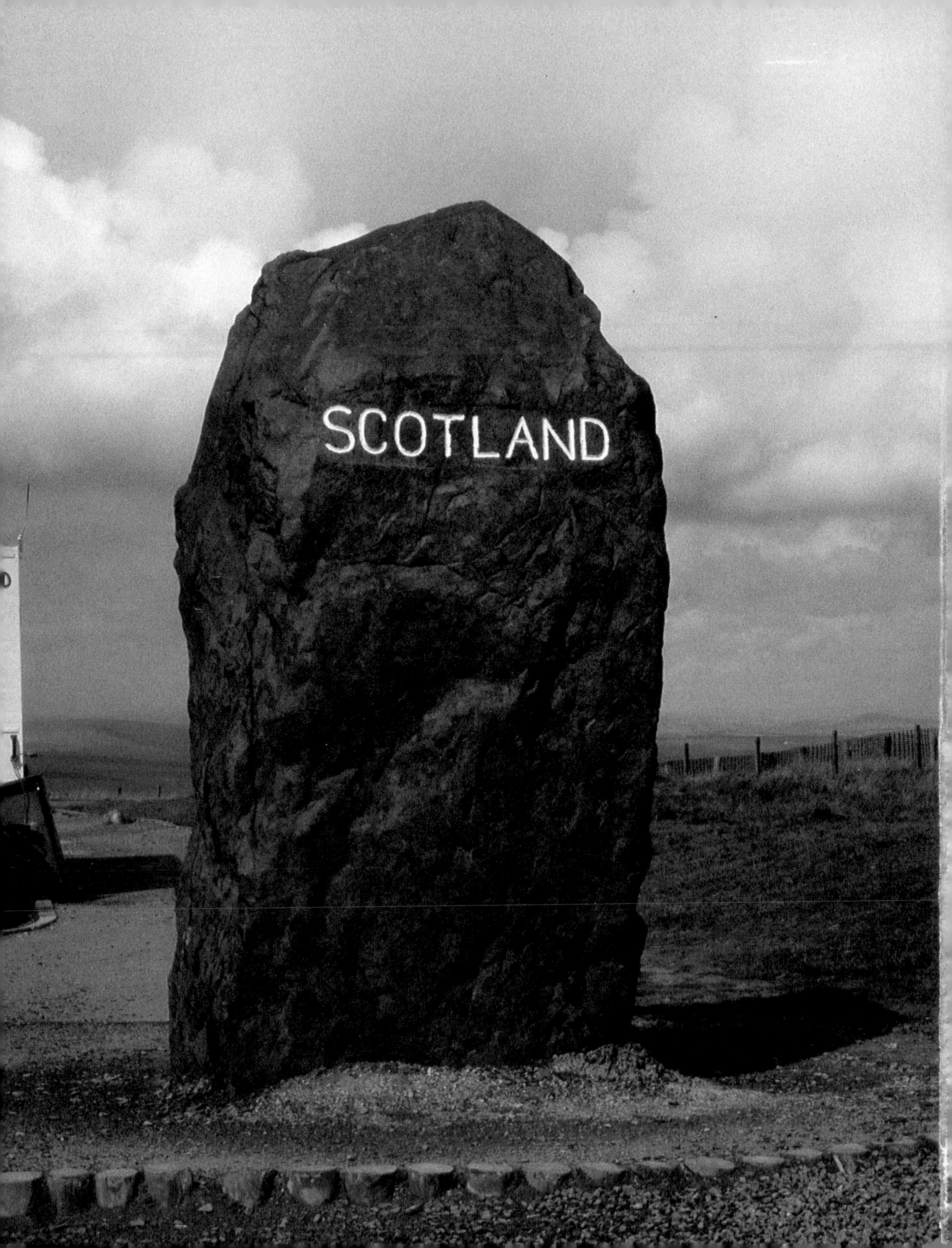
SCOTLAND

CLASSIC
TOURING ROUTES
IN SCOTLAND

ADRIAN GARDINER

LOCHAR PUBLISHING · MOFFAT · SCOTLAND

© Adrian Gardiner, 1991

Published by Lochar Publishing Ltd
MOFFAT DG10 9ED

British Library Cataloguing in Publication Data
Gardiner, Adrian
   Classic touring routes in Scotland.
   1. Scotland – Visitors' guides
   I. Title
   914.1104859

ISBN 0–948403–60–8

Typset in 10 on 12pt Garamond No. 49 by
Chapterhouse, Formby and printed in Great Britain
by Eagle Colourbooks Ltd., Blantyre, Glasgow

Maps by Hawthorn Graphic
Design by Mark Blackadder

INTRODUCTION

When I meet someone, halfway around the world, who admits to never having been to Scotland, I feel deeply, deeply sorry for them. Despite the pervasive influence of what the writer Kenneth Roy describes as a 'junk "international" culture', Scotland is still largely unspoiled. Its routes, compared with those of England, are uncluttered and it is one of the few remaining parts of Europe where motoring is actually a pleasure.

There is an inherent risk in writing about travel. Recommend a little-known beauty spot to the world at large and the idyllic can quickly become plastic with discarded wrappers and litter. I have taken this risk because Scotland is big enough to cope. The sensible traveller will remember he is a guest and the wise guest does not upset his host. The sensible traveller will note that the Scots are a hospitable race, and though 'Westminster' is a dirty word in many places, they do not bomb Harrods or torch holiday cottages. There are few Scots who do not try to live up to the humanitarian example set by their national poet, Robert Burns, and that in itself makes Scotland a great country to travel in.

We are going on a journey right round Scotland on 'classic routes' – the Great North Road, the Road to the Isles, the royal route through Deeside and many others. We are going to meet some heroes and some villains. We are going to see some wonderful architecture and some blots on the landscape, for the educated traveller of today is interested in both. We are going to see the physical remains, thousands of years old, of lost cultures. We are going to visit remote coastlines and the last refuges of rare birds like the golden eagle and the osprey, and declining species like the otter and grey seal.

This book is addressed to the consumer. Its length requires that much has been dealt with in outline, for Scotland is a vast country with a long history and a wealth of legend and folklore. To paraphrase Dante: 'My long theme drives me on so urgently that words must often fail to match the facts.' We hope not.

I have referred to Robert the Bruce in the shorter modern form of Robert Bruce, and similarly have occasionally abbreviated the National Trust for Scotland to NTS.

ADRIAN GARDINER,
Gifford,
Scotland, 1991

Acknowledgements

I should like to thank the many people around Scotland who send me information, news and press releases. More specifically, I have been fortunate in having Leslie Gardiner, a writer before I was born, at my elbow. Not only has he put his vast knowledge of Scotland at my disposal, he has also painstakingly corrected my text.

Nearly all the monochrome pictures were taken by Kevan Coulton, who came to Scotland in his wheelchair for the purpose.

The offices of Historic Scotland, 20 Brandon Street, Edinburgh, kindly supplied pictures as did the Highlands and Islands Development Board of Bridge Street, Inverness. I am also indebted to the following: Inveraray Jail Museum; Cally Fleming at Nevis Range; Brian Nodes of Blair Castle; Gordon Davidson; and to Carol Ann Ward at United Distillers for pictures.

The remaining photographs are from the author's collection.

AG

Contents

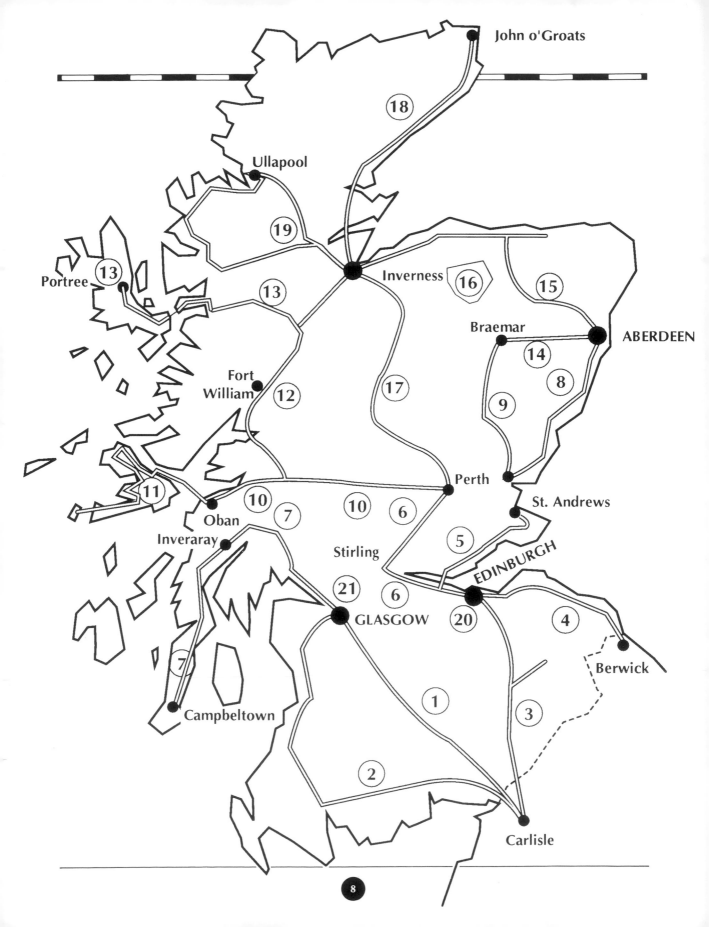

1

GRETNA TO GLASGOW
A74 AND M74

This is the busiest route into Scotland. For the next ten years it may also be the slowest, as the sixty-eight miles between the M6 and M74 are upgraded to

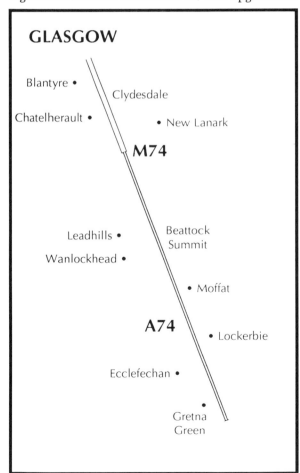

GLASGOW

Blantyre •

Clydesdale

Chatelherault •

• New Lanark

M74

Leadhills •

Beattock
Summit

Wanlockhead •

• Moffat

A74

• Lockerbie

Ecclefechan •

•
Gretna
Green

motorway standard. That is, assuming the Scottish Office get their way. Perhaps it will be the last motorway built in Britain: attitudes in the 1990s are changing. A new logic is emerging. The opening of the M25, humorously referred to as Britain's biggest car park, made no visible difference to congestion on the north and south circulars. You have plenty of time to wonder, sitting in three lanes of stationary traffic, where all these cars and coaches and articulated trucks were before.

Build a road and miraculously it fills up with vehicles. In truth, we are hopelessly addicted to the American Dream; armed with a Divine Right to boldly take our cars wherever we want, whenever we want. Would the £500 million (certain to be more at the end of the day) be better spent on public transport? It is a question for politicians. Undoubtedly the A74 is a dangerous highway: sightlines are poor and, as on the A1 in north Yorkshire, traffic turning right has to cross two lanes of oncoming vehicles which rarely adhere to the speedlimit. The solution is simple and economical: a strictly-enforced 50 mph limit. Like Mr Toad, we are obsessed with speed. Life is not really that short.

WEDDED BLISS FOR
COACH PARTIES

It *is* too short to waste time on Gretna Green. That coach-load of French tourists is assembled to watch two of their number going through a mock-marriage ceremony and by the time they have finished another coachload will have arrived. Gretna Green is a shabby

THE MOFFAT RAM: a symbol appropriate to the Scottish Borders, where sheep outnumber people by at least 100:1.

NEW LANARK: meticulous restoration of Robert Owen's Utopian mill village where the doctrines of socialism began.

introduction to a beautiful country, as John o' Groats is a shabby finale.

We might stop at Ecclefechan instead and give a boost to the visitor statistics at Thomas Carlyle's birthplace museum. It is the least frequented of the National Trust for Scotland's (NTS) properties, though among the most accessible. But Carlyle's star declined below the horizon many decades ago. To the Victorians he was the archetypal 'lad o' pairts', the deprived boy who, like David Livingstone and Andrew Carnegie, made his way to the top through the Scottish virtues of stubbornness and tenacity, of 'porridge and the Shorter Catechism'.

The cottage is a good example of eighteenth-century rustic architecture, arranged around a pend (archway) which connects front to back. Carlyle's father built the place with his own hands.

Seven miles back, the worst accident in railway history – 220 dead – occurred to an overcrowded First World War troop train. Seven miles ahead, and seventy-three years later, 270 died when the fireball of a bombed 747 jet landed on a petrol station in Lockerbie, the worst disaster in aviation history.

MOST BEAUTIFUL SCOTTISH TOWN

Now the A74 begins imperceptibly climbing, tracing the Annan river to its source. Hills like thunder-clouds are massing ahead of us. Are we in the Highlands? Not by a hundred miles, but two villages here – Leadhills and Wanlockhead – are the highest in Scotland.

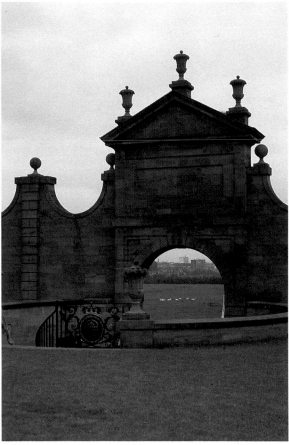

CHATELHERAULT: former hunting lodge of the Dukes of Hamilton, set in a country park.

Neither from highway nor from the Euston-Glasgow railway do you see anything of Moffat, which is only two miles off the route but low-built and lodged in the bowl of the hills. People discover Moffat by accident, then start going there for their holidays. Technically just outside the Borders, it shares all the Borders' amenities – golf, fishing, pony-trekking and hill-walking – but none of the Borders' strident chauvinism. No claustrophobic wynds or obstructive tolbooths decorate Moffat. Its broad sloping esplanade must be the most spacious high street in Scotland.

They used to call it the Cheltenham of the north, a slightly fanciful comparison, but Moffat does have healing water and a curative air. People tread the same path that Boswell and Burns trod to the Moffat Well, descend the same steps under the stone cupola and drink from the same spring . . . then hurry back to the Town Hall to report that sewage is polluting the Well. It's the natural taste of a cure worse than many diseases, the taste officially described in the handouts of two hundred years ago as 'somewhat resembling rotten eggs beaten up in the scourings of a foul gun'.

Though virtually a New Town on the Scottish timescale, Moffat has a few historic hotels, including the Star, which appears in the *Guinness Book of Records* as the narrowest free-standing hostelry in Britain. Chapel Street behind it is supposed to be Britain's shortest street. The town is poorly equipped with tartan trinket shops. Pressure to promote the Bonnie Scotland image is something the local council pig-headedly resists. The town is sadly deficient in bingo halls and Chinese takeaways. Shops and cafés belong to an age of elegance that, elsewhere, very old people may just remember. If you have a taste for furniture, quality woollens and handcrafts there are discoveries to be made. If you have a sweet tooth, Moffat toffee is made, sold and exported by its inventor's great-grandson.

Between June and October Moffat is an overflowing basket of flowers. It's a three-times winner of the Britain in Bloom contest, has twice recently been voted Best-Kept Village and holds the Most Beautiful Scottish Town trophy. Do bear Moffat in mind when you travel along the A74.

CRADLE OF THE CLYDE

Climb out of Moffat and you are soon back on the Glasgow road, which now proceeds to a considerable altitude. (For a view of the Devil's Beef Tub, the 'deep, black, backguard-looking abyss' of Sir Walter Scott's *Redgauntlet*, the 1000-foot hole where old-time rustlers gathered their stolen cattle, continue for two miles up the Edinburgh road.) The main railway line is beside us all the way, but we don't race the trains as we did in the days of steam. For the old night express this ascent of Beattock was a weary climb, punctuated by stops and starts, guaranteed to wake you up. Then daylight flooded the landscape and the train picked up speed, hastening into a quiet watered land of emerald and gold.

Since electrification, the Inter-City takes Beattock in its 100-mph stride. The summit behind us, it's all downhill to Glasgow, the sun lighting the pastures and the heather and black pinewoods rolling away. Over to the right, on the regional boundary, three major rivers spring from one hillside: the Annan, going south; the Tweed, going east; and the Clyde, going north. A Glasgow journalist traced the Clyde to its source on Clyde Law and jammed a cork into the stone pot from which it bubbled, then he returned to Glasgow with visions of a dried-out river bed and all the ships lying on their sides. When he got there he found everything going on as usual.

Clydesmuir has become Clydesdale, several mountain streams have collided and the young Clyde, swift-rolling over a pebbly bed, sets its course

for Glasgow. Shall we make one last detour before we leave the moorland heights, and take the short steep road to the twin capitals of the *montagnard* enclave, Leadhills and Wanlockhead? There isn't much to see: the birthplaces of Allan Ramsay, the first popular poet, and of William Symington, first of Scotland's dynasty of marine engineers; the highest golf course in Britain; the grave of Mr Taylor, Britain's longest-lived person, under an illegible slab in the village cemetery; the Hall of the Mountain King itself, a labyrinthine disused lead mine, open for guided tours. That's about all.

DREAMS OF UTOPIA

Soon after we pick up the motorway we leave it, to return to the Clyde at New Lanark. We think of the crèche for pre-nursery school children as a modern concept. It is not many years since the leather tawse was banned as an instrument of discipline in schools, following a case which went to the European Court of Human Rights. And workers' holiday funds and contributions to health care are generally assumed to be twentieth-century inventions.

Not so. Step forward Robert Owen, a man two hundred years ahead of his time. A young Welshman, he came to New Lanark near the end of the eighteenth century and married the daughter of the boss, David Dale, overcoming considerable opposition. On the latter's death he inherited the largest cotton mill in Europe. It may seem harsh to us today that Owen employed children aged six and seven to work thirteen hours a day – but in the climate of the Industrial Revolution Robert Owen and David Dale were attacked as traitors to the mill-owning class, and Owen may be considered the father of universal education.

'I know,' he said at the opening of his Institute for the Formation of Character in 1816, 'that society may be formed so as to exist without crime, without poverty, with health greatly improved . . . and happiness increased a hundredfold.' At New Lanark, Owen discarded the punishment/reward system, believing knowledge came from nurturing the senses. Lessons at his school included singing, dancing and nature study. His novel method of discipline was the 'silent monitor': each child kept a four-sided, four-coloured wooden block. The side displayed uppermost indicated the child's conduct, and the miscreant who showed black would suffer the taunting of his peers. Owen's other reforms prompted William Morris to write, eighty years later: 'The doctrine of socialism has its origins in the social experiments of New Lanark.'

Today the village of New Lanark, saved from the bulldozers in 1975 by its Conservation Trust, is not only a memorial to Robert Owen, not merely a World Heritage site, but a living community once more. In 1990, after the expenditure of some £30 million, the project is about two-thirds complete. A state-of-the-art exhibition centre has opened: a monorail rides past lasers, holograms and 'talking heads' called the Annie McLeod Magical History Tour. Annie, a ten-year-old fictional mill worker, describes her lifestyle. There are acres of Grade A listed buildings. The mill lade is being cleaned and repaired and there are plans to have the machinery working by water-power again. The Clyde rushes by in a torrent of waterfalls.

THE DUKE'S HUNTING LODGE

We follow the A72 north on a converging course with the motorway. Between the mileposts of garden centres along the Clyde Valley we see the river disappear and reappear. Is that one of the packhorse bridges Coleridge and Wordsworth enthused over? Are those the crystal linns (rapids) where J. M. W. Turner set up his easel? We cross the motorway, ignoring it, and stay on the Hamilton road.

Hamilton Palace, more grandiose than any palace Scotland's monarchs knew, has vanished without trace. Erected by one duke on the profits of coal, it sank under the feet of another, undermined by that same coal. But their hunting lodge, a palace in miniature called Chatelherault, survives in the middle of a country park, while at the foot of the hill the imaginative adventure playground is a favourite of local schoolchildren.

Chatelherault is a solid reminder of the Auld Alliance, the historical pact between Scotland and France – two nations which had little in common but their dislike of England. Upstairs in the duke's apartment above the fireplace is a modern allegorical painting of the 2nd Earl of Arran playing political chess. Governor of the young Mary, Queen of Scots, he holds her poised above the chessboard, her future in his hands. The other pieces on the board represent the royal families of England and France: the earl is plotting the political and financial future of all three countries. Henry II and Catherine de Medici, ultimately parents-in-law of Mary, rewarded Arran with the title of Duc de Chatellerault (*sic*).

It is a time-warpy kind of place. Stand at the open window of the duke's apartment with your eyes closed and you can almost hear the sounds of galloping hooves, hunting horns and the baying of hounds. Perhaps you can see James, the 5th Duke of Hamilton, spurring on his horse to cut off the stag. Now open your eyes. We are back in the twentieth century. Beyond Hamilton the motorway curves the final miles into Glasgow on the horizon. It is time to move on, but first we award Hamilton District Council full marks for a meticulous restoration which has catalysed our historical hallucination.

BLANTYRE, WE PRESUME

Last stop, about six miles from Glasgow, is the industrial village of Blantyre, built as a fortress-town of the Middle Ages would have been built, within the loop of the river. Encased in that smart, country-house style building we expect to find the miserable but-and-ben (cottage of one room and an outhouse) where David Livingstone was born into extreme poverty.

The expensive renovation includes some good commemorative sculpture in a courtyard bounded by a museum, a library and an African studies centre: the place to go if you are wondering what it was exactly that the missionary achieved. Not very much, seems to be the answer. He led a full life, if daily exposure to danger, discomfort and ill-health constitutes a full life. We can put him ahead of some of Scotland's more loudly-sung heroes, because Livingstone was a man of steady courageous energy, the quality that all the world admires.

2

GRETNA TO GLASGOW THROUGH BURNS COUNTRY

Seven miles after the M6 becomes the A74, turn on to the A75 for Annan and Dumfries. You are now on the road to Ireland although the ferry ports of Stranraer and Cairnryan are a hundred miles away – a fact not always appreciated by motorists when they calculate their journey times. This historic highway consequently sees a fair amount of reckless driving. For the most part, even when it is embroidering the beautiful Galloway coastline, it is a succession of

straights and well-engineered bends and by the time this book appears the notorious bottlenecks of Annan and Dumfries will have been set to one side. The dog-legged streets of these old burgh towns where two vehicles could hardly pass without colliding will have been replaced by broad bypasses where three or four vehicles can all collide together.

We are heading west from the cul-de-sac of the Solway Firth, Britain's most useless inlet for

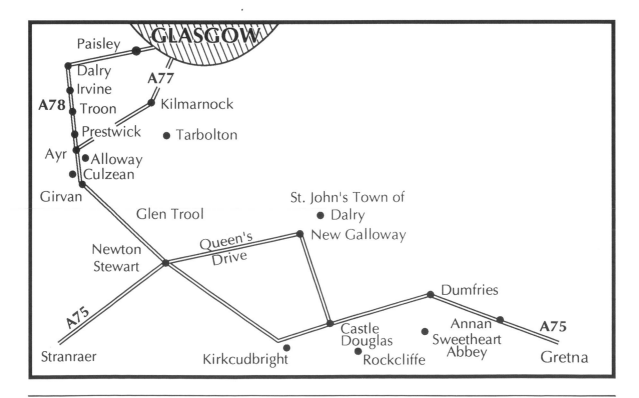

navigation. Here, and not on the Cheshire shores, are those Sands of Dee where Mary fatally called the cattle home. Port Mary, beyond Dalbeattie, commemorates another Mary: the Queen of the Scots who said farewell to Scotland at that point and stepped aboard the boat which carried her to England, to half a lifetime of imprisonment and to her execution.

Other places on the Solway shore have 'port' in their names: an optimistic designation. Ripping tides, shallows and shifting sands make the upper firth a nightmare for pilots. A hundred square miles of the Solway Firth look ripe for reclamation. Perhaps somewhere in a regional surveyor's drawer are plans for 'Solway City', a conurbation designed to cover what is now mud, water-meadow and estuaries between Annan and Carlisle. One hopes not, because Britain's marshlands, habitat of unique wildlife, are fast disappearing. Not that the Solway is altogether a blank page in maritime history. Some of the clippers of the tea and grain races last century carried Annan as their port of registration. They were built in that apathetic one-street townlet three miles from the sea: under tow, gliding down the narrow canal-like Annan river, they must have appeared to be sailing across dry land.

BURNSIANA

Annan has a few old sandstone buildings. Robert Burns lodged there towards the end of his life: he was a customs and excise officer and the harbour was his beat. (The house is now the Café Royal.) Later there was a railway bridge across the Solway to Bowness in Cumbria, with a 197 piers sunk in Solway mud. Ice flows struck it a mortal blow in the phenomenally cold winter of 1881, but another fifty years went by before the wreckage was cleared. More recently Annan has had the privilege – if that is the word – of receiving Scotland's first nuclear power station at Chapelcross.

Eight miles from the sea, Dumfries has no maritime air but was once a seaport like Annan. Shopping malls have replaced the shabby wynds and vennels of yesteryear. The Greyfriars' monastery chapel, where Robert Bruce took the first steps to the throne by murdering the Red Comyn, is now a

supermarket cellar under Castle Street. It is a hard life for the antiquarian in modern Dumfries, but perhaps much of its gloomy history is best forgotten anyway.

Dumfries lies at the end of the Burns Trail (he died here); it is a good place to start on the poet and work backwards to Ayr. The Dumfriesians were among Rabbie's earliest admirers: they made him a freeman in 1787, before his works had reached a wide public. Then, as a resident of the town, he embarrassed everyone with his drunkenness, his unpredictable behaviour and his left-wing politics. (But it was a fellow poet Campbell who, at Dumfries, shocked the burghers by proposing a toast to Napoleon – which was rather like someone in 1940 proposing a toast to Hitler. 'Do not mistake me,' said Campbell. 'Napoleon is a monster, I agree. He is the enemy of the human race. But never let it be forgotten that Napoleon once shot a publisher.')

Burns relics in Dumfries include his last home; the Globe Inn where he caroused; his ornate mausoleum and the more recently established Robert Burns centre. On the Burns Trail (map from local tourist office) you can pick up the farms he unsuccessfully cultivated like Ellisland and topographical associations like sweet Afton, the brigs of Ayr, bonnie Doon and the braes of Ballochmyle; haunts of his rampageous youth around Mauchline and Souter Johnnie's cottage; and his birthplace and ostentatious heritage centre at Alloway. Our classic route passes close to them all. Don't bother with Maxwelltown, suburb of Dumfries. The district is full of Maxwells and the braes immortalised in *Annie Laurie* are fifteen miles away above Moniaive, where Annie's ancestral home Maxwelton (*sic*) House, now an agricultural and folk museum, is worth a visit.

A POOR PIGEON

So who was Burns? English people have viewed the cult of the Bard with amused tolerance: another example of the Scots, whose literary and artistic record is pathetic, inflating the reputation of the best of a poor bunch, a moderate-sized fish in a very small pool.

To the Scots, on the other hand, he is rather more than the greatest poet who ever lived. He is the lover of noble causes, the champion of the underdog,

THE ARROL ASTER: car-building was a major industry in Dumfries in the 1920s; the thirties recession wiped it out.

the exposer of hypocrisy and self-esteem, the prophet of a compassionate society undreamed-of in his day.

We should accept this view of Burns, because as time goes by it appears that the Scots have it more nearly right than the English. His dialect poems, which non-Scots consider too obscure to wrestle with, mask the purest and smoothest stream of lyrical talent. He was a rake. He had the manners of a lager lout. But his poetic genius drew out the 'tears of things', his simple quatrains are unrivalled for sweetness and sadness:

> *Oh, wert thou in the cauld blast,*
> *On yonder lea, on yonder lea;*
> *My plaidie tae the angry airt,*
> *I'd shelter thee, I'd shelter thee.*

When Scots around the world gather on Burns Night (25 January) to honour him, the Bard is among the company in a way that Shakespeare or Dante could never be. For all his genius, he remains 'one of

us'. His murky love life and sordid end evoke a profound psychological response even in the most pompous pillars of society – the 'unco guid', he called them – who have always abounded in Scotland. As he lay dying, aged thirty-seven, a 'poor pigeon hardly worth the plucking', a citizen of Dumfries asked 'Who dae ye think'll be oor poet now?' It is a question, *pace* McDiarmid, the Scots are still asking.

FOUR-WHEEL BRAKING

Our route from Dumfries is west and north. There are worthwhile detours south or along the coast road through Kirkcudbright and Creetown. This countryside is the location of two well-known thrillers: *The Thirty-Nine Steps* by John Buchan and *Five Red Herrings* by Dorothy L. Sayers. When the latter was televised a Dumfries-built motor car came out of its retirement in a museum to play the part of the police car. A less-well-known aspect of

SWEETHEART ABBEY: impressive sandstone shell founded by Devorgilla; a legend of marital devotion.

Dumfries's history, the Arrol factory had a prolific output in the early part of this century. Its Galloway car, as seen on TV, was built by an all-female workforce, had a top speed of 50 mph and cost £325 when it appeared at the Scottish Motor Show in 1926. Its big brother, the 1909 Arrol Johnston, was the first car to have four-wheel braking. It is preserved in Melrose motor museum; a Galloway and a very rare Arrol Aster (1928) are a Myreton museum near North Berwick.

SWEET, SILENT COMPANION

South of Dumfries in the village of New Abbey stand the ruins of one of Scotland's finest Cistercian abbeys. Sweetheart Abbey was founded in 1273 by Devorgilla, a distant cousin of Robert Bruce, in memory of her husband John Balliol. In a romantic if slightly macabre legend, she had his heart embalmed in a silver and ivory casket which she carried around with her: her 'sweet, silent companion'.

SCOTLAND'S CANNIBAL TRIBE

From the mini-yachting centre at Kippford – just a chandler's, a post office and the inevitably-named Anchor Hotel – a coastal path takes in some dramatic views. In the estuary of the River Urr a causeway leads to Rough Island, a NTS bird sanctuary. But beware: the causeway is covered at high water and the tide comes in, as local wisdom puts it, 'faster than a galloping horse'. And swim here at your own risk. We are only thirty miles from Sellafield as the mutant crow flies, and frequently plutonium levels are recorded here which are sixty times normal background level.

South of Rockcliffe, the coastal track passes close to the Bogle Hole. This roofless cave has been suggested as the *pied à terre* of Sawney Bean, infamous sixteenth-century cannibal, though some authorities argue for another cave at Bennane Head, south of Girvan.

By the time Mr Bean and the forty-odd members of his family were arrested, they had murdered and eaten over a thousand travellers. In their bone-carpeted cave the bodies of men, women and children were hung up like strips of dried beef. Retribution was savage. Those caught red-handed, under Scots law at the time, were not allowed the luxury of a trial. The men of the tribe had their limbs severed and were bled to death, watched by their women who were then burned in the manner of witches.

COVENANTERS' STONES

Back on our route we come to Castle Douglas. You will look hard for a castle (*six* red herrings?) until you come to Threave, a mile out of town. The square keep has an ideal situation on an island in the river; but the surrounding gardens are better known. Here the NTS runs a two-year residential course in horticulture. A network of unobtrusive tarmac paths without steps makes Threave no problem for disabled people.

Lakes come thick and fast as we turn for New Galloway. They are the riverine lakes of the Loch Ken hydro scheme, artificially landscaped and decorated with little barrages. Pause at the head of Loch Ken, at the knot of villages set in hollows by junctions of interconnecting lanes. Dalry – properly St John's Town of Dalry and the prettiest village in the area – and Balmaclellan kirkyards hold a wealth of Covenanters' graves with their typically blunt inscriptions, reminders of an era of religious persecution as brutal as anything that goes on in Belfast or Beirut. At Balmaclellan there is a monument to Robert Paterson, the 'Old Mortality' of Scott's novel, who wandered through the south-west tidying up the martyrs' graves.

Much sentimental ink has been spilled over the Covenanters. They could be seen, like their persecutors and like terrorists and bigots of all eras, as a fanatical extremist minority, themselves committed to violence.

THE CRANNOG OF CLATTERINGSHAWS

The Queen's Drive, from New Galloway to Newton Stewart, is truly a classic route. The Forestry Commission is a major landowner in the area and the scenery is best appreciated in autumn. Relics from the

mud at the bottom of Clatteringshaws' lake inspired the reconstruction of a crannog (prehistoric conical-roofed dwelling) in the field behind the Deer museum. Is there something inherently suspect about the idea of a deer museum? It reminds you of the Joni Mitchell song:

> *They're gonna take all the trees*
> *and put 'em in a tree museum;*
> *and charge all the people*
> *a dollar and a half just to see them.*

Six miles on, park under Murray's monument and try the breathless climb to the viewpoint. You have a wonderful vista of jumbled heathery hills, the very essence of Galloway; and on the obelisk you can read the inspiring history of Alexander Murray, a shepherd lad whose intellectual brilliance prompted the local laird to give him an education. Murray was already professor of Oriental Languages in Edinburgh when he died while only in his thirties.

South-west Scotland's highest mountain, Merrick (2764 ft), towers over Glen Trool as we take the wild hilly road to Girvan (A714). We are in a vast tract of lake and moorland called Glen Trool Forest Park – but some find the heavy conifer afforestation monotonous and are relieved by the sight of the smiling little valley just over the watershed, welcoming them to Ayrshire. The isle of Arran is in view, and closer at hand the 1000-foot granite sugarloaf of Ailsa Craig. Ocean-going ships out of the Clyde set a course at Ailsa Craig which they don't need to alter until they are off Finisterre, 1000 miles away.

'THE WHIMSICAL BUT MAGNIFICENT CASTLE OF COLLANE'

Now we are on the Golf Coast, a chain of well-known golf courses of which Turnberry, dominated by its barracks-like hotel – 'commodious' is the official description – is the queen. Commodious also is Culzean, the most-visited NTS property in Scotland.

When Robert Adam died in 1792 he had completed the Castle, the Clock Tower Court, the

PAISLEY TOWN HALL: reflected in a department store window opposite the leaning Abbey.

Ruined Arch (built as a Gothic folly), the Gazebo and the Dolphin House. The owner's successor, Captain Archibald Kennedy (who came home from a rather fashionable address: 1 Broadway, New York) and his descendants added a few more trappings of gracious living: the Pagoda, Gas House, Hoolity Ha', the Orangery and a Fountain Court. The pick of the bunch must be Adam's Home Farm, a splendid complex of buildings forming a square within an octagon. Culzean has many unique features including the original grand entrance to the castle: the Cat Gates, whose leopards are made of Coade stone, a composite whose recipe died with the Coade family.

The castle's interior has the architectural novelty of an oval staircase which culminates in an Oval Presidential Suite. Top floor apartments reserved for General Eisenhower and his descendants were the nation's thank-you to a great war leader. As they toil up the staircase, visitors hear the voice of

Vera Lynn, the music of Glenn Miller and the polished perorations of Churchill floating down from the Eisenhower Presentation, a pot-pourri of Second World War memorabilia swirling through screens of battle flags, medals and combat jackets. It is tacky. It is nostalgia at its most heavy-handed.

Culzean was a latecomer to the numerous cliff-top castles of the Ayrshire coast, though its owners, the Kennedys, involved themselves fully in local activities from medieval times. A hooligan named Kennedy persuaded a local abbot to part with some property by 'roasting him in sope'. Successive Kennedys by similar ploys acquired a large slice of Ayrshire coastline and got themselves ennobled. The first earl fell at Flodden. The second died in a brawl on Ayr sands, the third was poisoned at Calais. In recent years litigation over property between the current Kennedy and his estranged wife has kept Sunday newspaper readers entertained and visitors flocking to the seagirt citadel.

SCOTLAND THE BRAVE

North of Culzean we come to Alloway where Burns spent the first seven years of his life. The birthplace cottage is now overshadowed by the ambitious Land o' Burns centre, with all the trademarks of the modern heritage business: souvenir shops, audio-visual presentations, tourist board office. We are also in the country of the patriot William Wallace, and the combination of Burns and Wallace has given Scotland a mediocre national anthem. The jerky tune and clumsy syntax of *Scots Wha Ha'e* do credit neither to composer nor to lyricist. The sentiments of *Scotland the Brave* are jingoistic by modern standards, while *Auld Lang Syne* has been hijacked for Hogmanay. It is curious that the Scots have never settled on an effective national song – particularly since Scots wrote *Rule Britannia*, the *Maple Leaf* and *Waltzing Matilda*.

Ayr, an attractive town with wooded residential suburbs where good hotels and guest-houses can be found, remembers William Wallace in its Wallace Tower and Robert Burns in its Auld Brig and Tam o' Shanter Inn. It also boasts the most sophisticated racecourse in Scotland, though competition from the other three or four is not severe.

KASHMIR SHAWLS AND PAISLEY HANDKERCHIEFS

Five miles from Ayr, British Airways trains its pilots at Prestwick. The commercial future of this little airport, designated in the 1950s as Britain's second international terminal, is in jeopardy. Thirty miles from Glasgow and sixty from Edinburgh, its road and rail connections are poor late at night and at weekends. Its proximity to the eastern seaboard of America is no longer a factor: modern passenger jets have a greatly-extended range.

As far as Ayr Bay the Clyde shore has been cold and unfriendly-looking. You are really astonished to hear of people coming here for their holidays. Beyond Prestwick, through Ardrossan and Largs, the countryside is more civilised. Parkland rolls down to the sea, which has an inviting sparkle. Yachts appear. We don't stay with the coast, nor with the A77. Though the latter is the shortest route to Glasgow, traffic on this highway is fast and furious at all times of the day and night.

The A78 takes us past Troon, another golfing mecca. Past Irvine, Scotland's answer to Blackpool, we leave the dual-carriageway for the A737 through another Dalry, this one the birthplace of Sir Alexander Fleming, pioneer of penicillin. On Glasgow's doorstep, Paisley is often overlooked. Its abbey (*c.* 1163) has a side which leans dramatically away from the perpendicular and very short opening times. Paisley is famous for its patterned shawls: the 'teardrop' motif originated in Kashmir and was copied from samples brought back by the East India Company. More mundanely, the handkerchief was invented here. The Museum and Art Gallery has some fine examples of shawls and other collections which make it second only to the civic museums of Edinburgh and Glasgow.

We can run into Glasgow past the Burrell Collection or, if going north towards Loch Lomond, take the Erskine Bridge across the Clyde.

3

LANGHOLM TO EDINBURGH THROUGH THE BORDERS, A7

For a dozen miles after you leave the top of the M6 on what is signposted the 'Edinburgh Tourist Route' the featureless plains have the character of a

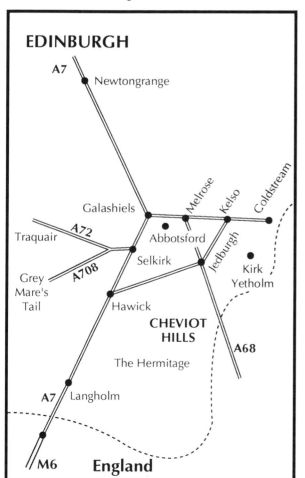

no-man's-land. Where Rivers Esk and Eden make their way apathetically to the sea, you feel you are neither in England nor Scotland. Then you pass the Saltire roadsign (Scottish cross of St Andrew) and the topography changes. You climb steadily towards the horizon, pine forests creeping ever closer to the road. Here is Langholm, the 'Muckle Toon' (muckle means big), with a few Jacobean-style houses, an appalling block of civic flats and, beyond the town, a broad sweep of parkland beside the River Esk: an idyllic picnic spot.

The ninety miles to the capital can safely be covered in two hours. There are long straights for overtaking summer caravans. The principal towns after Langholm – Hawick, Selkirk and Galashiels – are not bypassed but not busy. Unless you fall foul of a Common Riding.

BRAW LADS AND LASSES

Even on this main road at the height of the tourist season the traveller may be obliged to join a queue of stationary traffic for an hour or two, while up ahead the Braw Lad, the Callant or the Cornet is flourishing his colours, assembling his cavalcade, and setting off on the annual circuit of the parish.

Common Ridings are the excuse for a dozen little Border towns, which for fifty-one weeks in the year look dour and unimaginative, to explode in pageantry and merry-making. Ostensibly the Ridings may celebrate the granting of a royal charter centuries ago, or some legendary affray where local heroes made their mark. Legendary in a parochial sense, of

GREY MARE'S TAIL: impressive waterfall and wildlife sanctuary in the heart of the Borders.

TRAQUAIR: one of Scotland's oldest dwellings; the Bear Gates have been locked since the 1745 Jacobite uprising.

course: the Galashiels Riding comes from a story handed down through the generations about some local lads who found English soldiers robbing an orchard and taught them a lesson. (Hence the town motto, 'Soor Plooms'.) But it is hardly *Il Palio*. Of the Braw Lad's Gathering, Magnus Linklater notes 'an element of middle-class gymkhana about it'.

After the turn-off to the Hermitage, a remote and eerie ruin with Mary, Queen of Scots associations, we pick up the River Teviot and cross it four times before entering Hawick. Not much to detain you here: the insular little town's chief claim to fame is the disproportionately high number of rugby players it supplies to the national team. The town hall with its crow-stepped gables is a foretaste of much baronial and pseudo-baronial architecture to come.

Whatever amenities the diminutive market towns on the A7 lack are compensated for by the charm of the countryside. A short and exciting switchback road with panoramic views leads us into Selkirk. The Flodden monument and civic museum are in the older part of the town, while down in the valley is an example of urban renewal. The deserted woollen mills are becoming homes to microchip factories and mushroom farms.

TWO CLASSIC DETOURS

Before we continue north from Selkirk there are two classic routes running west. Crossing the river and turning left on the A708 we pass Bowhill, stately home of the Dukes of Buccleuch, and follow the Yarrow Water up to St Mary's Loch, a notable beauty spot. The road – whose ultimate destination is Moffat – skirts the loch past Tibbie Sheils, a historic drovers' inn frequented by Sir Walter Scott and the Ettrick shepherd, James Hogg.

Shepherds are not much in evidence today, though the hills are alive with the Blackface sheep and in April and May this unfenced road is alive with their lambs too. Drive with care: there are more than a million of Scotland's most popular breed and most of them are just round the next corner, sitting in the middle of the road.

A few miles on, the silver streak high up on your right is the Grey Mare's Tail. For the energetic, there is a NTS footpath to the top of this impressive 200-foot waterfall. But keep to the path. The Tail has a sting: there have been four fatalities and numerous injuries.

Our other detour from Selkirk is to follow the River Tweed alongside the A72. Another NTS venture, one of their newest, is at Innerleithen where for a century until recently the Smail family ran a jobbing printers. The daily guardbooks show records and proofs of every dance-hall ticket and wedding invitation and, because of the advent of computerised typesetting, machinery at Smail's in use ten years ago is now a museum-piece.

At Innerleithen or perhaps Walkerburn you may encounter your first mill shop. There are many more farther north and they are a notable Scottish scam, capitalising on Scotland's reputation overseas for all things woollen. Coach drivers are paid a fat commission – tax-free cash in back pocket – to bring coachloads of tourists into the huge car parks. Whether you consider this is bribery or just the enterprise culture in action, note that over 90 per cent of raw wool is now imported, and in any case the link between Tweed, the river, and tweed, the cloth, was the result of a misprint – the word 'tweel', which means twill, being corrupted to 'tweed' by a firm in London.

THE BEAR GATES

Just along the road is Traquair, said to be the oldest continuously-inhabited dwelling in Scotland. With its small-scale rooms and passageways the house has great charm and in summer there are falconry displays and craft fairs in the grounds. Traquair has its own brew-house and Traquair Ale, strong and dark, is bottled for sale. If you want a souvenir of Scotland to take home, you could do worse than to buy a bottle or two. Drive the perimeter of the estate and you will see the Bear Gates. They have been locked since 1746 and

will not be opened until a Stuart monarch sits on the throne: a constitutional improbability.

From Selkirk through another mill and market town, Galashiels, the last forty miles of the A7 drop out of heather and sheep moor to the plains of the River Forth. On the outskirts of Edinburgh we pass Lady Victoria colliery (a mining museum at Newtongrange) and the Butterfly Farm. But our final detour is not north, but east into Scott country.

HANDSOME STATION AND INCONGRUOUS PILE

Four miles from Galashiels, Melrose is the jewel in the Borders' crown. Described as the handsomest provincial station in Scotland, Melrose station includes a good cafe and craft shop, model railway displays and periodic exhibitions. The renovation is the work of a local architect, though at the time of writing the building is on the market so its future purpose is uncertain. Over the river in Gattonside, the Hoebridge restaurant is one of the country's best; from the cheerful and inexpensive Marmion's bistro we can walk to Melrose Abbey, one of four massive ruins in the area. The others are at Kelso, Dryburgh (where Scott is buried), and Jedburgh. (Jedburgh is the birthplace of Sir David Brewster, inventor of the dioptic lens and the kaleidoscope. A true Scot, he agreed to be knighted in 1831 only after he received a royal assurance that the usual fee of £109 would be waived.)

The area is rich in stately homes. They include Mellerstain, near Gordon, and Floors, on the banks of the Tweed outside Kelso, where *Tarzan of Greystoke* was filmed. Abbotsford, just outside Melrose, probably attracts more visitors than either of them.

'The most incongruous pile that gentlemanly modernism ever devised,' wrote John Ruskin of the dilapidated farmhouse which Sir Walter Scott turned into a baronial castle. Few read Scott today: his novels are turgid by modern standards. 'I've spent better nights with haemorrhoids,' commented Scots comedian Billy Connolly. You cannot go far in the Lowlands without meeting some reference to Scott. Statues of him dominate prime sites in Edinburgh and Glasgow city centres. He has much to answer for in promoting tartanitis and the vulgarly romantic aspects of Scotland. Worth a visit on a clear day is Scott's View where, legend has it, the horses pulling his funeral carriage stopped of their own accord.

THE SORCERER'S APPRENTICE

From Scott's View we look out over the Eildon Hills. According to legend they were supposed to have been split into three by Scotland's equivalent of Merlin, the twelfth-century wizard Michael Scot. But the Romans knew this place as Trimontium. A stone near the A68 marks the site of their fort and a long-term programme of excavation is beginning.

In a story which has parallels with the *Sorcerer's Apprentice*, the wizard (whose unmarked grave is said to be in Melrose Abbey) leaves his trainee with an agenda of menial tasks. The bored student of magic decides to enlist the help of his master's goblins and discovers, too late, that once they have been released they must be kept fully occupied or they will start destroying the world. The desperate youth, unable to control them, eventually orders them to make a rope out of sand: in theory, an impossible task.

The fanciful story has a sinister postscript. Centuries later in 1942 the first quartz (sand) threads were made, and in the same year the Atomic Energy Authority was set up to administer the awesome new invention of nuclear fission.

GIPSIES AND DRAGONS

Downriver we go to Coldstream and cross the Border to visit the site of the battle of Flodden. 'The flowers o' the forest were a' wede awa'' goes the verse, the 'flowers' being King James IV and most of the Scottish nobility, massacred by the English army in 1513. We can take the B6352 to Kirk Yetholm, for centuries the home of the Faas, a gipsy clan. The last queen, Esther Faa Blyth, died here in 1883. Hereabouts the Pennine Way begins: the long-distance footpath ends 230 miles away at Edale in Derbyshire.

Before you reach Kirk Yetholm, note on your right the depressions on Linton Hill. They are supposed to have been caused by a dragon, the Worm of Wormistone, and there is a stone carving in Linton church which depicts a man with a falcon fighting a dragon. The legend is an old one: around 1174 John Somerville, the Laird of Laristone, was appointed Royal Falconer and Baron of Linton as a reward for saving the villagers from the Worm.

Worms and wizards, Soor Plooms and the Stuart kings: the Border region is a land rich in myth and legend.

MELROSE STATION: disused and carefully renovated, the 'handsomest provincial station in Scotland'.

TRIMONTIUM: parallel to the A68, the viaduct spans the River Tweed beside a major Roman fort.

BERWICK-UPON-TWEED
TO EDINBURGH, A1

In the days of horse-drawn public transport the Great North Road from London to Berwick was furnished with inns at intervals of ten miles or so, where you could eat, drink, sleep, stable your horse or hire a carriage. North of the Border the situation was different. The fifty miles from Berwick to the outskirts of Edinbrugh was served by three dismal little dram-shops. Respectable people hardly cared to enter them. Those who did encountered the typical disobliging Scottish innkeeper whose 'provoking indifference' to the needs of the traveller – usually cold, wet, weary or all three – is emphasised in many nineteenth-century diaries.

Things haven't changed all that much. Until he crosses the Tweed, the northbound motorist has a reasonable choice of hotels and eating places, some of them those same old coaching inns. After that there is little until you come to Cockburnspath. At

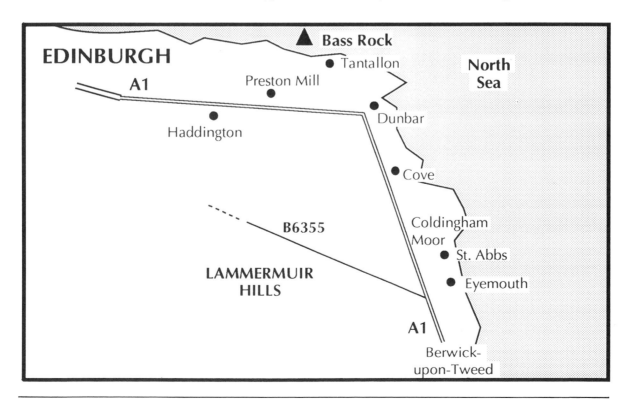

Cockburnspath, in the so-called hotel, the bar is set out with bottles and the till is ringing merrily. But ask for a meal or a snack or even a cup of tea and the manager will explain he is too busy serving drinks. To let you understand, as the Scots say, the place is owned by a brewery and his job depends on increasing turnover and to make sandwiches at five in the afternoon for strangers would simply not make sense. His regulars wouldn't stand for it. (This conversation takes place beside a dangerous bend on the A1, often referred to in the press as a 'killer road'. Drink is a factor in most of its accidents.)

We're tempted, then, to go non-stop from Berwick to Edinburgh. The only towns, Dunbar and Haddington, are bypassed; the final stretch from Tranent is virtually a motorway; if we allow an hour for the journey we will not be far out.

AT WAR WITH RUSSIA

Berwick-upon-Tweed is also bypassed. From the graceful new bridge over the Tweed you can look downstream to the town's three older bridges, which include the stone bridge with packhorse embrasures, built to facilitate the travels of James VI of Scotland when he became James I of England in 1603; the Royal Tweed bridge which replaced it in 1928; and the dramatically-curving railway bridge, in which George Stevenson incorporated the sign: THE FINAL ACT OF UNION. Five miles upstream stands another Union bridge, suspension-type, which carries a lane from nowhere to nowhere.

There are two well-known facts about Berwick. One, the town is still at war with Russia over the Crimean question. (Constitutional documents used to refer to 'England, Scotland and Berwick-upon-Tweed' but no one signed for Berwick at the Paris peace treaty of 1856.) Two, the town has been six times Scottish and seven times English. Nowadays it is in England, though north of the Tweed, and if the polls which are carried out are any guide, the inhabitants intend that it shall remain so. Just north of the town, west of the A1 as it enters Scotland, is the battle site of Halidon Hill (1333). Note the date: nineteen years after Bannockburn. At Halidon Hill the English bowmen took ample revenge for Bannockburn but forebore to exploit the advantage.

EYEMOUTH: flourishing fishing harbour, one of a dozen which have survived.

From the Border the A1 runs parallel to the main rail line, between the eastern escarpments of the Lammermuir hills and the cliffs of the North Sea. Side roads descend on severe gradients to diminutive fishing harbours and villages which have length but no breadth, squeezed between cliff and sea. Burnmouth is an example; so is the flourishing harbour of Eyemouth.

FRESH FISH FROM THE QUAY

Running down to Eyemouth in a characteristic dean (steep narrow valley choked with foliage) of the Berwickshire corniche, the last half-mile of the Eye Water is broad enough to be canalised and on a sunny

within yards of the harbour and no family escaped bereavement.

If you have detoured to Eyemouth, take the old road over the moor to rejoin the A1 near Cockburnspath. Rarely concerned with topographical accuracy, Scott should really have called his novel *The Bride of Coldingham Moor*. These days people are more familiar with Donizetti's opera *Lucia di Lammermoor* than with the novel which inspired it. But in the latter, the rock-fortress and quicksands of 'Wolf's Crag' can be identified with the ruins of Fast Castle on the coastal footpath. Ravenswood, the principal *mise en scène*, was an imaginary building located somewhere near the high point of the moorland road. The whole tragic tale is taken from an event in Scottish history which belongs not to eastern, but to south-western Scotland: the 'tricky and mean-spirited' Sir William Ashton was modelled on the first Viscount Stair, one of the Galloway Dalrymples.

HIGHEST CLIFFS ON THE EAST COAST

' . . . Seventeen miles; one thousand and ten; falling more slowly . . . ' – St Abb's Head, a few miles from Coldingham village, is one of the Meteorological Office's principal weather stations, as featured in BBC shipping reports. The site is important not merely to mariners, but to historians (St Ebba built a chapel here, destroyed by the Danes in AD 870) – and to naturalists. The cliffs are one of the NTS's largest open sites and provide impregnable nesting places for thousands of sea birds: kittiwakes, guillemots, razorbills and many others.

The National Trust for Scotland is a curiously hybrid organisation. Critics point to its 'teashoppiness'. You *know* the well-spoken ladies who show you round have a select collection of hats reserved for Sundays. But the Trust's policy of buying up large tracts of coastline and wild places is admirably in the public interest, since it protects the environment from unscrupulous property developers and builders of nuclear power stations.

Naturalists and those in no hurry to reach the capital would benefit from a detour inland and miss two gigantic eyesores and a road often dangerously over-trafficked. From Grantshouse turn left towards

day it reminds you of a Sicilian port. In Scottish waters the herring fishery has declined, the benefits promised by EC membership are not yet apparent and some of the traditional bases of the Scottish fishing fleet (apart from Eyemouth they were Buckie, Macduff, Peterhead, Fraserburgh, Lerwick, Ullapool, Oban, Mallaig, Campbeltown and Ayr) look to be in terminal decay. But Eyemouth survives, with working boats at the quay and a healthy smell of fish at the docks and the frame of a new vessel (is she to be a trawler or a yacht for a sheikh?) rising on the boatyard stocks.

In 1981 they opened a fishery museum in Eyemouth. It was the centenary of a major tragedy: the whole Eyemouth fleet was wrecked in a storm

COVE: former smugglers' harbour; an idyllic place.

Duns and right at Preston on to the B6355.

This minor road goes through the middle of the Lammermuirs. Few strangers penetrate these wildernesses. When they do, they realise they are entering a last refuge of wildlife. The sudden noises which startle them as they spread their rugs on the turf and listen to the silence are the trill of the curlew, the wail of the plover, the rackety squawk of the grouse, the intermittent dialogue between ewe and strayed lamb – those, and maybe the splitting roar of a supersonic fighter, to remind them they are still in touch with civilisation. The whole line of the hills is a low-flying exercise area and, typically, the end of the Cold War seems to have doubled the frequency of these exercises.

Low-flying is a major menace over nine-tenths of Scotland. It affects not only the long-suffering residents: there are frequent letters in the press from people whose holidays have been ruined. From the tip of Caithness to the Mull of Galloway the Ministry of Defence and its hot-rod pilots appear to ignore the regulations governing minimum flying heights. Eyewitness reports put aircraft as low as forty feet. Complain and the MoD sends you a silly leaflet with idiotic drawings.

SMUGGLERS' HARBOUR

Back on our main route: just after Cockburnspath, on the right is the sign to Cove. Follow the road past the former coastguard cottages to the car park. You can go no farther by road: there *is* one, but the sandstone is slowly crumbling into the sea and the local authority has declined to continue repairing it, preferring instead to use their funds to extend their ugly headquarters in St Boswells forty miles away.

Cove harbour was gifted to the County Council (subsequently the Regional Council) in the 1970s. The Region then sold it to a property developer from England in 1989. The developer later insisted the purchase was conditional on developmental planning permission, which the Council denied. Lawyers for the estate which made the original bequest pointed out that the Council had no authority to sell it anyway.

Don't let this classic case of bureaucratic mismanagement put you off visiting Cove. It is a magic place. The tiny harbour, once a smugglers' haunt, is now rarely used – the entrance is narrow between submerged rocks and its use depends on almost perfect weather conditions – but it is much visited for its clean white beach and clear water.

This first thirty miles into Scotland is a grim introduction to the country. Here is the squat concrete of Torness nuclear power station, built with the aid of massaged statistics from the South of Scotland Electricity Board (now ScottishPower) and the dithering of the local planning department. There, five miles on, is the spreading virus of a cement works.

Note the sign to Oldhamstocks, one of many hamlets off the main road, nestling under the hills. Here, around 1750, lived a joiner named Broadwood who walked to London to get a job making piano crates and ended up the foremost piano maker of his day.

There is little left of the castle above Dunbar harbour – though ten miles on round the coast there is a fine ruined sea-fortress at Tantallon – but Dunbar's suburb Belhaven is home to one of Scotland's few small breweries. Belhaven ales are available in Edinburgh and other parts of Scotland, but connoisseurs come here to drink them at source. Dunbar pubs are rather dour: the Battleblent hotel is the top of the range.

INTRODUCING JOHN RENNIE

Some miles on, the A1 bypasses East Linton. It is worth turning off for Preston Mill, one of the NTS's flagships. It is said to be the oldest working water-driven meal mill in the country (sixteenth century), and the lopsided pantile-roofed kiln is a favourite with photographers and watercolourists. A short walk away stands Phantassie Doocot, large by any standards for a pigeon house. The walls are four feet thick.

It was at Phantassie around 1780 that John Rennie, marine and civil engineer, served his

TORNESS: the nuclear power station is an unnecessary blot on the landscape, and a grim introduction to Scotland.

PRESTON MILL: 16th-century water-driven meal mill, still in working order.

apprenticeship with Andrew Meikle the agricultural machinery pioneer. Rennie went on to build docks in London, naval dockyards at Chatham, Portsmouth and Plymouth, and bridges across the Thames, including Waterloo bridge.

TREASURE ISLAND

The conical hill to the south of East Linton is Traprain Law, an extinct volcano. Some claim it as one of about twenty-two possible sites of King Arthur's Camelot. From the prehistoric stone circle on top of the law you can see to the Firth of Forth: the island of Craigleith was R. L. Stevenson's model for *Treasure Island*. The 'sugarloaf' to the right is a volcanic plug, the Bass Rock: from North Berwick there are boat trips round it in summer to view the nesting gannets, while cormorants wheel around the boats in the harbour. (Rumour has it that cormorants have

appeared on London restaurant menus as 'Highland chicken'.)

Take care on the last section of the A1 after East Linton. There are unmarked blind summits, lunatic overtakers, heavy day-trip Sunday traffic and an average of a death a week. The whole route from Morpeth should have been upgraded to dual-carriageway years ago.

Stevenson's grandfather designed these eastern approaches to Scotland's capital city. He intended travellers to see the hills draw aside like theatrical curtains until the romantic stage-set, lion head of Arthur's Seat, Castle Rock and clustered spires, was revealed in all its splendour. Motorists today slide into Edinburgh on the new mini-motorway, the first landmarks being superstores and a DIY emporium. But even today you have a view of Arthur's Seat, presiding over Dun-Edin, the fort where Edinburgh began.

5

EDINBURGH TO ST ANDREWS BY THE EAST NEUK

Small rivers in large towns usually become main drains and garbage tips, and the Water of Leith is no exception. Some effort has been made to clean it up where it enters the city centre at the West End, and a footpath has been established. From the footpath and from Dean Village, in Victorian times a complex of tanneries, you can appreciate the grandeur of Thomas Telford's Dean Bridge, two hundred years old and as good as new, and also reflect on the lost

charms of that little waterway as it trickles amid dense foliage under the 120-foot Randolph Cliff.

The Dean Bridge is our exit from Edinburgh on the road to Queensferry and Fife. When Telford was around this was the city limit, but his bridge opened up a large and attractive area for urban expansion and for four miles we travel through some of Edinburgh's most desirable residential suburbs.

There is nothing unobtrusive about the two

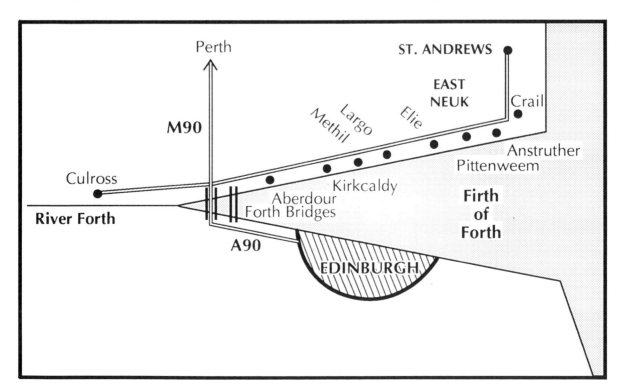

FORTH BRIDGE: the eighth wonder of the world; climax of Victorian triumph over nature's obstacles.

famous bridges which cross the narrows of the Queensferry Passage, ten miles from Edinburgh. Every detail is visible to the watcher on the shore. The road bridge, a mile long and opened in 1964, is of the modern suspension design, indistinguishable from a dozen built over estuaries in Britain and abroad in the past thirty years. The railway bridge, a mile downstream and a mile and a half long, is unique. Superbly photogenic, visible for miles upriver and down, its three great cantilevers and monolithic pillars still proclaim Victorian values: determination to overcome every obstacle nature could put in our way.

TEREBINTH AND TURPENTINE

Described at its opening in 1890 as the 'eighth wonder of the world', the Forth Bridge's monumental scale becomes apparent as you descend into South Queensferry. The town has become a quiet backwater since the last ferry ran in 1964. It boasts historic Hawes Inn, featured in Stevenson's *Kidnapped*. A cantilever towers above you, the height of the dome of St Paul's in London. At regular intervals a toy train rattles its way across. 'Painting the Forth Bridge' still has its proverbial application to a never-ending job – the popular myth is that it takes three years and then it is time to start again. In fact it is inspected every six years and a team with spray guns carries out necessary maintenance. The formula for the paint is unchanged since the day the bridge was built: red lead, iron oxide, linseed oil, terebinth and turpentine. A definitive history is by Anthony Murray and in fiction the structure has inspired clever symbolism in Iain M. Banks's novel *The Bridge*.

LITTLE HOUSES AND BIG SUBMARINES

Coming off the road bridge at North Queensferry the exit road is signposted 'Fife Tourist Route' and first-time visitors must get more and more puzzled about

CULROSS: unusual wall-mounted sundial. Even the electricity sub-station in the town is a listed building.

it as they drive the dreary ten miles to Kirkcaldy. It is the price we pay to reach the coast beyond: the East Neuk, King James IV's 'golden fringe of a beggar's mantle'. Before we turn east we might make a short detour in the opposite direction. Skirting the naval base of Rosyth, where nuclear submarines are refitted and where radiation levels many times the national average are recorded, we pick up the road to Culross (pronounced 'Q-russ'). The little town is an architectural feast. Even the tiny electricity sub-station is a historic listed building.

The Royal Burgh of Culross was founded in the sixteenth century and became a flourishing port, trading in coal and salt. Aside from the whitewashed cottages with their crow-stepped gables and low doorways, the character of Culross comes from its steep cobbled streets. The flat flagstones in the middle were reserved for the gentry: the proletariat were confined to the edges. The National Trust for Scotland has had a proprietary interest in the town for fifty years, has restored a similar number of buildings and has a reception centre in the town hall.

THE BLACK RIVIERA

Along the coast to Kirkcaldy you need not keep buckets and spades at the ready. Apart from pockets of sand at Aberdour, Pettycur and Largo this is a black riviera. The currents which scoured out the bays left deposits of sea-coal and dross from ancient mine workings higher up the river. The coalmines of Fife (the last one closed in 1989) ran down to the coast between Kinghorn and Leven, and often continued under the sea. Methil, in its heyday, had more foreign consulates than any town in Scotland.

We no longer know from the reek of linseed oil that we are within three miles of Kirkcaldy: linoleum's halcyon days are over. Today's reek is of tar: the A92 is habitually punctuated by roadworks, a manic painting-the-Forth-Bridginess. The main street along the seafront, featureless and interminable, gave Kirkcaldy the nickname 'The

CULROSS: only at Culross and Banff has Scottish 16th-century civic architecture been so well preserved.

Lang Toun'. It used to be a noted seaport: until recently you could identify the passenger landing-stage and read leftover advertisements for passages to London, all found, for around £2 or £3. Adam Smith, the guru of monetarism, was a native of Kirkcaldy and his father, the local Customs Collector, earned enough to educate his son at Balliol College, Oxford. Another Adam, Robert Adam the architect, was born in the vicinity.

ISLAND CASTAWAY

At Lower Largo there is a monument to Robinson Crusoe. Alexander Selkirk, on whom Defoe's novel is based, went to sea not as a fisherman like his brothers, but as navigator in a privateering expedition: a freelance pirate. In October 1704 arguments began with the captain of the *Cinque Ports* and, with no faith in the seaworthiness of a ship riddled with Spanish shot, Selkirk insisted on being put ashore. The nearest land was the island of Juan Fernandez, 400 miles off the coast of Chile.

He was found there four years and four months later by Captain Rogers of the frigate *Duke*, who described 'a man clothed in goat skins, who looked wilder than the first owners of them'. The rest, as they say, is history. But history does not record the titles of Selkirk's eight favourite gramophone records.

HERRING AND WHALING

Pittenweem, Anstruther, Elie, Crail: each little port used to be a shrubbery of masts and rigging, hemmed in with sandstone cottages whose very pantiles were impregnated with the smell of fish. The main street is usually Shore Street or Shoregait, a cobbled water-front abutting on a square basin fortified with massive low walls. The houses, planted on steep twisting lanes, have toy gables, toy dormer windows and outside stairs in the old Scottish manner, and nowadays colour-washed facades. Decorative carvings in worn sandstone, scarcely legible now but meant to represent anchors, ships and the like, surmount the lintels like hostelry signs in the medieval quarters of European towns.

The professional fishermen, like the fish, have mostly moved on. The harbour walls are no longer festooned with cordage and nets or piled high with lobster creels. But the little harbours and bays are finding a new life in the leisure industry, and the fresh breezes are agreeable to windsurfers.

Here on Shoregait, where boatyard workers park their white hatchbacks (the builders of the traditional blunt, broad-beamed little 'Fifie' fishing boats are into yachts and motor cruisers now), cadgers in blue bonnets once argued over prices, then galloped away with cartloads of fish for half the towns of eastern Scotland. Fishwives plodded after them in voluminous striped skirts, bowed under wicker baskets. 'Eight thousand barrels you'd see stacked on that quay,' says one ancient mariner, 'and five hundred lassies and laddies packing them with herring fresh-drawn from the Firth.'

MINISTERS, MONKS AND THE DEVIL

Unless this walnut-faced longshoreman is pulling our legs, strange taboos persist. Rats, hares and rabbits are not mentioned in the fishing fraternity. Neither are pig, salt, salmon or minister. Circumlocutions have to be found: 'red fish' for salmon, 'yon chap from the manse' for the minister. A visiting preacher innocently took 'Ye are the salt of the earth' for his text and throughout the sermon the congregation was bent as in prayer, grasping 'cold iron' under the pews to ward off evil.

Pittenweem ('place of the cave') incorporates in its harbour walls the cell of St Fillan the Celtic monk. Crail has a famous Blue Stone with the Devil's thumbprint on it. According to legend, he sat on the Isle of May offshore and took aim at Crail church with a boulder. One half remains in the square where it landed and the other half rolled down to the shore. His thumbprint is on that half too, proving he needed two hands to lift it.

Anstruther is the East Neuk's metropolis. There are notable seafood restaurants in the area. The Scottish Fisheries Museum exhibits the frames and blueprints of traditional boats, log-books and souvenirs from the Arctic voyages of the whaling skippers last century, and the freaks and monsters recovered from their trawls. Nostalgia for some; for others a tangible reminder of a lost era, an era almost unimaginable as you drive through the sleepy villages prettified by the National Trust for Scotland.

The greatest event in Anstruther's history, only vaguely documented, occurred in December 1588 at five in the morning. 'Sir,' reported the Reverend James Melville's servant, 'I haiff to tell newes. There is arrived within our herbris a schippe full of Spainyarts, but not to giff mercie but to ask it.' These stragglers from the Armada had been rescued from the Fair Isle between Orkney and Shetland and brought south by an Anstruther fishing smack. They stayed some weeks in the East Neuk and, once the locals had discovered they were human beings like everyone else, they fitted in well and by all accounts were sorry to leave.

SEEING THE LIGHT

Six miles off Crail, where we turn for St Andrews, another piece of maritime history sticks up out of the sea. Few people land on May Island except by accident. Sailors used to discover it the hard way. Excepting the 'Round O' of Arbroath Abbey, its beacon seems to have been the first in Scotland. King Charles I allowed two Lothian men to build it in 1635 and to collect dues from passing shipping. It was no more than a coal-fired brazier tended by three stokers. Seafarers objected to being charged for a bonfire which, they alleged, was more smoke than flame and easily confused with burning lime-pits on the shore. Improvements must have been made as time passed because when the Commissioners of Northern Lighthouses took it over at the end of the eighteenth century they paid the Duke of Portland £60,000 for it.

What is the future of Britain's lighthouses? Sophisticated satellite systems navigate tankers round the world's coastlines, as they guide aircraft to within a hundred yards of an airport eight thousand miles away. Lighthouses are expensive to maintain. Though most countries consider safety a matter of public interest to be funded out of general taxation, Britain charges shipping companies Light Dues. As charts and compasses are replaced by computer banks and digital displays, and lighthouses are rationalised – extinguished – the losers will include thousands who sail Britain's coastline not for profit but for pleasure. (Recently an automated lighthouse in the Hebrides was converted into holiday accommodation, becoming the first licensed lighthouse in Britain.)

PRIM MAIDEN AUNT OF SCOTTISH TOWNS

'No one seems to dispute the world's most widely-practised game originated in Scotland five centuries ago,' wrote Sir Harry Boyne. But the Dutch have an equally valid claim to the invention of golf. What *is* a fact is that the Royal and Ancient Club (R & A) at St Andrews proclaims itself the world governing body of the game. Commenting on press reports that the Soviet Union was building golf courses, the Secretary of the R & A said 'If the Russians want to play golf, they will have to approach us first.' St Andrews is one of the few clubs modelled on the English system of privilege: generally the game in Scotland is neither élitist nor class-conscious and visitors find the numerous courses invigorating and inexpensive.

St Andrews has a newly-opened golf museum, a sea-life centre, broad streets, a couple of good wholefood restaurants, the oldest university in Scotland (whose cycling students will remind you of Cambridge), and a ruined castle and cathedral. Legend has it that five bones and a tooth of the apostle Andrew are buried under St Andrews Cathedral. A monk, Regulus (anglicised as Rule), was instructed in a dream to collect them from the saint's place of martyrdom at Patras in Greece. Rule dreamed his way across Europe, each night's vision showing him the next day's journey until he arrived at what is now St Andrews and settled down to convert the heathen Picts.

Legend also says, without any historical evidence, that Andrew was stretched on a decussate (X-shaped) cross; hence the design of Scotland's flag.

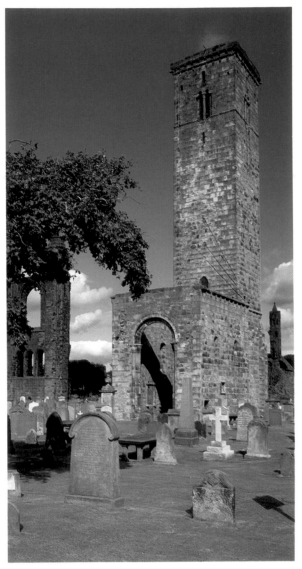

ST RULE'S TOWER: legend says Rule, guided by dreams, brought the bones of St Andrew across Europe and buried them here.

The St Andrew's cross is not exclusive to Scotland. The armies of Tsarist Russia, ancient Scythia and nineteenth-century Hungary and of the Confederates in the American Civil War all fought under it.

As to the bones, since 'authentic' skeletons or bones of St Andrew are displayed in Istanbul, Amalfi, Notre-Dame in Paris, Tournai and Aix-en-Provence, it seems just possible Rule got hold of the wrong ones.

6

EDINBURGH TO PERTH BY STIRLING

For those who are hurrying to the Highlands there is a perfectly good motorway from the Forth Bridge to Perth. There is another perfectly good motorway to Stirling and we shall see little of that either. The first half of our classic route follows more closely the narrowing Forth estuary and most of it is signposted 'Forth Valley Tourist Route'.

Compared with England, the redevelopment of Scotland's disused industrial transport systems –

canals, and the railways which made them obsolete – is at an embryonic stage. The cleaned-up ten-mile stretch of the Union Canal has not yet filled up with twee narrow-boats like the canals of Shropshire and Northamptonshire. The Edinburgh Canal Centre, based at Ratho (just before the roundabout where the Glasgow and the Stirling motorways divide), has a couple of floating restaurants and a little fleet of canopied boats for hire. The long-term plan is to

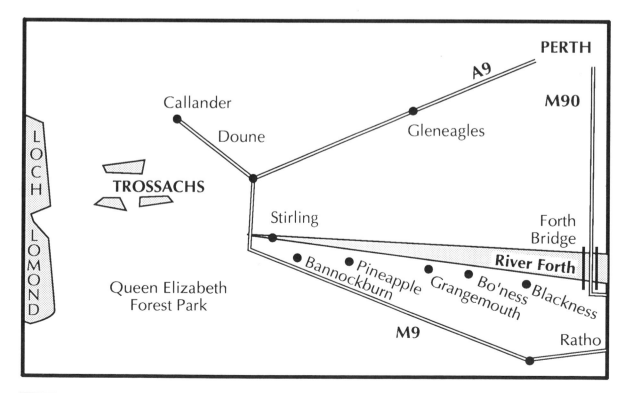

open up the whole length of the canal from Edinburgh to Glasgow. This will take some time: a housing estate has been built over it on the western fringes of Edinburgh while in central Scotland the canal runs through culverts, the cheap option for road builders.

From Ratho roundabout we head towards the Forth bridges and turn west on the A904. The enormous deer park at Hopetoun makes access to the nearby Firth difficult. Hopetoun House is vast too, vast and overbearing, the Adam style at its most grand. Almost next door, the House of the Binns looks almost cosy by comparison, though it was built as much for defence as domesticity.

ALAS, POOR YORICK

The most rewarding short detour on this coast is to Blackness Castle. The pugnacious fortress, unimproved since the sixteenth century, pushing its ram bow into the Forth, has been state prison, powder magazine and youth hostel in its day. Its present role, which is to be empty and not much visited, suits it best. A walkway runs atop broad defensive walls surrounding a keep and a film unit has recently shot scenes for a new production of *Hamlet* here.

This is a route of contrasts. The tourist on this 'Tourist Route' will be an intrepid one. The central Scotland area got the sharp end of the Industrial Revolution and urban decay north of the Border has an extra dimension of dreariness which makes Oldham and Barnsley appear reasonable places to live in. We enter Bo'ness (Borrowstoneness) through a landscape of rusting gasholders, dripping gutters and potholed pavements; past shabby low-rise flats with gang-slogan frescoes and boarded-up windows and, occasionally, a heavily-fortified video shop or takeaway.

Like some other towns of the Central Belt, Bo'ness is the kind of place where Rottweilers walk in pairs for safety and it was an act of rampant optimism to have included it in a 'Tourist Route'.

The justification is that Scotland has little to offer in the picturesque steam-railway department. It has nothing like the Dart line in Devon or the Bluebell line in Sussex. Here in Bo'ness is one of

BLACKNESS: prison of Mary, Queen of Scots on the River Forth; recent version of *Hamlet* was filmed here.

Scotland's two steam-railway centres (the other is farther north near Aviemore) of any significance, where volunteers of the Scottish Railway Preservation Society restore locomotives and renovate the tracks. You may see No 44871, known to afficionados as 'Black Five' and Lady Victoria, a former colliery shunter.

PARAFFIN AND PINEAPPLES

Some miles inland near Bathgate, James 'Paraffin' Young was born. The father of the oil industry also had plans, a hundred years ago, for a Channel tunnel. Grangemouth, a few miles along the coast from Bo'ness, is one of Europe's largest oil refineries: mile after mile of cooling towers, massive pipes and metal ducting. It has atmosphere: that of a vision of hell. 'Not only is the nearby River Carron badly polluted,' wrote Linklater, 'but the sheer accumulation of noxious and explosive substances in one place is a risky proposition.'

A more agreeable folly is near Airth, passing the longest swing bridge in Europe at Kincardine.

GRANGEMOUTH: 'sheer accumulation of toxic substances is a risky proposition.'

Remarkably little is known about the splendid Dunmore Pineapple. The architect's name is a mystery and the building (1761) is not mentioned in the journals of eighteenth-century travellers.

It is an exquisite replica. The stone leaves and scales of a central turret surmount a long high wall, originally the supporting wall of a glass hot-house – the decorative urns on top conceal chimneys. Pineapples and exotic vegetables were probably grown here in the days before refrigerated container ships. The large walled garden is being restored as an open site by the National Trust for Scotland. You can even rent the Pineapple as a unique holiday cottage. (Not from the NTS but from a company in England!)

1314 AND ALL THAT

The landscape to Stirling has a look of neglect, the lopsided look of abandoned mining country. By some, the mean-looking villages are taken as a symbol of the spiritual bankruptcy of a nation. But in the middle of them rises a symbol of national inspiration, Scotland's proudest memorial. On what

was accepted centuries ago (perhaps wrongly) as the site of the battle of Bannockburn, is a prominent celebration in metal and concrete of that fracas in 1314 which the Scots remember above all with national pride and self-determination. The exhibition hall, shop and cinema inside; the equestrian statue of Bruce outside (three-legged from almost every angle), are fairly new.

Perhaps the whole complex including the outdoor auditorium – some architect's dreadful parody of a prehistoric stone circle – will look better when it has weathered and the trees have grown round it.

Here the Scots secured a decisive victory over the auld enemy and the Bannockburn spirit resurfaces tirelessly whenever politics or football is being discussed. The Scots are entitled to their triumph. Against an enemy ten times her size there are few such triumphs in Scottish history. But the extravagance of displays like Bannockburn might prompt the visitor to wonder whether tribal jingoism – the wild optimism before the conflict, the whingeing self-pity in defeat, the prolonged gloating

THE PINEAPPLE: folly built in 1761, but much of its history and the name of the architect is unknown.

in victory – is altogether appropriate on the brink of the twenty-first century and in the face of the 'One World' theory. The English have done nothing so ostentatious at Flodden. They more than atoned for Bannockburn on Flodden Field where there is a stone, such as you might trip over, inscribed 'To the brave of both nations'.

We move on to Stirling Castle, the best-looking of the major Scottish strongholds, and the prize for the victor at Bannockburn. The complex of buildings crammed on the apex of the rock is sufficiently evocative of its savage history, and also touched with the Frenchified decorative features of the old Scottish style. Arrange if you can to visit the ramparts at dawn or at sunset on a clear day: the wonderful view to the west includes distant mountains like Ben Lomond and Ben Ledi which appear to move into the middle foreground.

The Wallace Monument (a slim tower) and seven battlefields are visible from here, confirming the castle's strategic importance. They include sites of notorious Scots-English clashes: Sauchieburn (away win), which ended with the murder of King James III; Bannockburn (home win); Sheriffmuir (drawn); and Falkirk, which the Jacobites claimed as a victory though it did not halt their retreat to Culloden. Of Falkirk, Major James Wolfe (later Wolfe of Quebec) said: ''Twas not a battle, for neither side would fight'. Despite the gloss which history paints over famous skirmishes, perhaps Wolfe understood the reality, when the rank and file who actually did the fighting had nothing to win and everything to lose.

CITY IN MINIATURE

No need to linger in Stirling itself, a place with traffic problems a town twice the size would be proud of. We can join the motorway northbound for a few miles to Dunblane. This little commuter town – or rather city, for Dunblane has a cathedral – is not

BANNOCKBURN: equestrian statue of Robert Bruce; Stirling Castle, the prize for the victors, is on the horizon.

much visited. The cathedral was a major target of iconoclasts at the Reformation but was carefully restored in the reign of Queen Victoria. John Ruskin considered it the best Gothic structure in Scotland.

THE BRISTLY COUNTRY

Before leaving Dunblane for Perth we might detour to Loch Lomond through the Trossachs ('bristly country'). Busy with caravans in summer, the road to Callander passes through Doune. A castle straddles an isthmus between two rivers near to Lord Moray's motor museum, a particularly aristocratic collection. The medieval bridge over the Teith has legendary origins: a ferryman refused passage to a poor tailor; the tailor served the king and grew rich and returned to Doune to build the bridge which put the ferryman out of business.

Staying with the A84, Callander is next. The 'Tannochbrae' of the television series *Dr Findlay's*

FAIR MAID'S HOUSE: stands on the site of the home of Catherine Glover, the 'Fair Maid of Perth'.

Casebook is a dignified market town for nine months in the year and a mecca of tourism for the other three. The long main street is thronged with thousands who have come to escape the city crowds. The new Rob Roy visitor centre is packing them in too, another desperate attempt to turn yesterday's dubious legends into today's hard cash. It is a piece of flexi-history. You can have the cattle-stealing, common criminal Rob Roy Macgregor, a villain for whom to feel sympathy, or the brave, daring, Robin Hood-style hero to be admired.

Only a step now, by lochs set in woodland and bracken like jewelled pins on a plaid of muted tartan, to the Trossachs. Busy as the road may be, there is still something mysterious about the approach. You feel you have penetrated someone's private estate and may shortly be asked to leave. The water is as clear as a tropical lagoon, the rocky outcrops have been meticulously sculpted by nature, the wooded islets float on mirror-images of themselves; dwarf oaks, rowans and silver birches twist out of the crannies like *bonsai* trees. The impenetrable botany has flourished since Rob Roy and his merry men declared it a no-go area 250 years ago.

From the steamer pier on Loch Katrine a little steam yacht backs off, turns and slips past Ellen's Isle. She is called *Sir Walter Scott*. (Scott's *Lady of the Lake* brought the first tourists flocking in.) For around sixty years she has been ferrying passengers to Stronachlachar and back, cruising on Glasgow's public water supply. From the Trossachs we can go on through Aberfoyle and the Queen Elizabeth Forest Park to Loch Lomond. But it is time to return to Dunblane and continue our journey to Perth.

THE GOLF GLEN

The A9, part single and part dual-carriageway, climbs steadily through Strathallan giving panoramic views of the Forth valley behind us. Perhaps Strathallan should be renamed 'Strathgolf' – no shortage of courses, though most of them seem to belong to Gleneagles Hotel. Modelled on a French château, with parterres and a landscaped park, Gleneagles was the most opulent of Scottish caravanserais, the prestige establishment of the railway companies in 1930 when it was new. It charged an outrageous eleven guineas a week per

person, full board.

The building has changed little, but the clientele has gone a long way downmarket. At over £100 a night, it attracts bookmakers and scrap metal tycoons. Once reserved for salmon-fishing, deer-stalking and grouse-shooting guests, the hotel has gone determinedly for the business-conference market, which naturally leads to greater emphasis on golf and equestrian schools, saunas and leisure centres. A private helipad has been added to the private railway station to which first-class Gleneagles Hotel sleeping cars once came direct from London.

FAIR MAID OF PERTH

Skirting the Ochil Hills, the railway, road and River Earn make their ways into Perth, the 'Fair City'. Two Bizet operas have relevance to Perth: one is *The Pearl Fishers*. The Tay bubbles through the town, trying to look like the Highland torrent it has been during most of its course. Downstream a few miles, where the Earn and Tay join, you once saw gipsies up to their waists in mud, feeling for mussels with their toes. Seed pearls the size of robin's eggs have been displayed in a Perth jeweller's.

The second opera is the *Fair Maid of Perth*. She was Catherine Glover and the present Fair Maid's House, itself over 300 years old, stands on the site of Catherine Glover's house. It is one of the best craft shops in Scotland, but don't expect to find tartan tammies and deer-horn ashtrays made in Korea. By the turret outside note the dirling pin, a medieval door-knocker. An earlier local heroine was Catherine Douglas. Nicknamed 'Kate Bar-Gate', she used her arm as a human door-bolt to give James I time to escape his assassins. (She was unsuccessful.)

Perth is a self-contained town; travel writers' favourite adjectives are 'douce' and 'genteel'. The Scottish Conservatives hold their annual conference here. We have searched for the red-light district without success. Safe and solid, Perth has plenty of green spaces, some fine bridges over the Tay, the famous Salutation Hotel where Bonnie Prince Charlie stayed, and an annual arts festival whose attractions are as diverse as *Don Giovanni* performed by Perth Festival Opera and the Glen Miller Orchestra (UK). Perth is a geographic nucleus too: classic routes fan out in all directions.

7

GLASGOW TO LOCHGILPHEAD BY INVERARAY

'Here is the house,' said Charles Rennie Mackintosh as he handed it over to Glasgow publisher Walter Blackie in 1904. 'It is not an Italian villa, an English mansion house, a Swiss chalet or a Scots castle. It is a dwelling house.'

The Hill House in Helensburgh is probably Mackintosh's best work. It does, in fact, incorporate a suggestion or two of Scottish baronial architecture, but the scale and proportions of the doors and windows are pure deco, a style in vogue across Europe twenty years later. Following an example set by William Morris, Mackintosh designed every fitting and fixture of the interior, from cabinets to keyholes. A true perfectionist, he delayed completion of Hill House for a year because of a strike at the Ballachulish slate quarry. He would accept no other shade of blue for the roof.

His wife, Margaret Macdonald Mackintosh, awaits to be 'discovered' by some feminist writer. She had a major influence on his style (which is characterised mostly by his unique appreciation of lighting, both natural and artificial) and nursed him through the final years of his life.

He died in obscurity in 1928. He had turned his back in disgust on the rigid and parochial ideas of the architectural establishment and spent the last dozen years of his life painting watercolours in France. For the next fifty years his furniture turned up in cheap salerooms, much of it ending up as firewood. In recent years his genius has been acknowledged and the city of Glasgow has several fine tributes to him.

Mackintosh is one of three pioneers we meet along the first stage of our classic route. We have already passed one: leaving Glasgow on the Great Western Road towards Dumbarton, we passed the monument at Bowling to Henry Bell. He

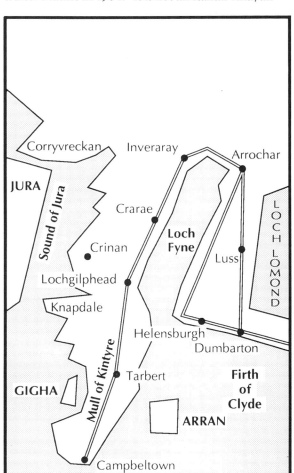

HILL HOUSE, Helensburgh: unique building by perfectionist architect Charles Rennie Mackintosh.

HILL HOUSE: features in the garden and the interior reflect the overall design concept of the house.

inaugurated the world's first paddle-steamer service from Glasgow to Greenock in 1812.

A LICENCE TO PRINT MONEY

Helensburgh, a short detour off our route from Dumbarton, is the birthplace of John Logie Baird, the television pioneer. His original equipment included several hundred torch batteries forming a two-thousand-volt power source, darning needles, string, sealing wax, piano wire, a tea chest and scanning discs made from cardboard. He seems to have had a turbulent career. Evicted from his Hastings laboratory after an explosion, he later had to bribe his frightened office boy with half-a-crown ($12\frac{1}{2}$p) to become the first person on television.

We could continue on this road to rejoin the A82 outside Arrochar. Periodical letters surface in the press from enraged locals complaining about the 'tinkers' caravans', for Faslane has a Peace Camp which looks out over the nuclear submarine base. The camp is hardly a blot on the landscape: for that you need look no farther than mile after mile of chain-link fence and huge 'MINISTRY OF DEFENCE: KEEP OUT' signs.

THE BONNY, BONNY BANKS

Retracing our steps, our first sight of Loch Lomond is by the village of Balloch where the pier is the berth of *Maid of the Loch*. She represents the end of an era, for just as Henry Bell's *Comet* was the first paddle-steamer built, so the *Maid* was the last. At the time of writing, restoration of the *Maid of the Loch* and sailings of her sister ship *Countess Fiona* have been suspended. Despite substantial investment from the public purse, the Australian company which owns the steamers and Balloch pier is in liquidation. Perhaps when a new buyer is found, the boats will carry sightseers again to Inversnaid at the north of Loch Lomond, past the piers at Luss and Rowardennan and under the shadow of Ben Lomond (3192 ft).

Luss, where the TV soap *Take the High Road* is set, is the only town of any size on the 'bonny, bonny banks'. Litter used to be a problem but recently this favourite weekend resort of Glaswegians has been smartened up. An exclusive country club with golf

LOCH LOMOND: paddle-steamer *Maid of the Loch* waits at Balloch pier for the result of legal wrangles.

courses and a yacht marina is opening its doors. Jet-skiers and windsurfers enliven the loch in summer.

We take the high road after Arrochar (turn left on the A83), a little fishing and boating centre at the head of Loch Long. Climbing on the modern road, you can see traces of the old one showing through the heather. It has been known for centuries as the 'Rest and Be Thankful'.

GEM OF SCOTTISH TOURISM?

Inveraray was a stopover on Dr Johnson's 'Grand Tour'. In 1773 at Inveraray Castle he first tasted whisky. Architectural purists consider this major Scottish stately home a rather absurd mixture of styles, and to describe the interior as ornate would be an understatement. It is the family seat of the Dukes of Argyll, the chiefs of the Clan Campbell, the history of which goes back to Gillespic Cambel, granted a royal charter in 1266. Over the centuries the Dukes of Argyll have also picked up the titles of Marquess of Kintyre, Marquess of Lorne, Earl of Campbell, Viscount of Lochow and Lord of Inveraray, Mull, Morven and Tyree. Had the second duke had the foresight to leave an heir, the family could have added the dukedom of Greenwich to the above list.

Sir John Vanbrugh, Roger Morris, John Adam and Robert Mylne all tinkered around with Inveraray Castle; John Adam (brother of Robert) also designed the two main buildings on the town's front, the Argyll Arms and the Town House. Inside, the castle has the usual sumptuous trappings of the ducal home including cannonballs from the Spanish galleon at the bottom of Tobermory Bay. Portraits of the Earls of Argyll hang in the Gallery: the seventh earl bears a striking resemblance to Blackadder of the cult TV comedy.

Sir Harry Boyne described Inveraray as a 'gem of Scottish tourism'. Some would say 'carbuncle'. Rabbie Burns was not impressed:

> *There's naething here but Highland pride,*
> *and Highland scab and hunger.*
> *If Providence has sent me here,*
> *'twas surely in an anger.*

FURIOUS RIDING

At least today's visitors are free to leave Inveraray. Thousands who got on the wrong side of the dukes were not. The Old Prison was opened in 1840, to be superseded by the New Prison eight years later. Both are now open as a major visitor centre. The guides are dressed as warders and prisoners of the 1870s and, in the oval courtroom, waxwork figures and an audio soundtrack portray a typical trial in progress. Reports on the inmates record draconian punishments for trivial offences: 'Furious Riding' for example, the equestrian equivalent of reckless driving.

Our road hugs the shores of Loch Fyne, famous for its kippers and birthplace of Neil Munro, whose fictitious hero Para Handy skippered his puffer – a coal-burning coastal boat – in these waters. As we leave the 'Duke of Argyll's Bowling Green', as the moors and mountains are ironically called, the landscape becomes more gentle and the vegetation more lush. Scotland's famous semi-tropical gardens on the west coast – Poolewe, Brodick Castle and others – owe their existence to both dedicated horticulturalists and to the Gulf Stream. Our road passes another at Crarae, where the azaleas and rhododendrons thrive on sandy soils and salt air.

CHUST SUBLIME

The Forestry Commission is a major landowner in this part of our route, which winds round to Lochgilphead between the forests of Knapdale and Kilmichael. 'Chust sublime!' says Para Handy, '. . . I would spend the rest o' my days in Lochgilpheid.' Apart from a rash of four-wheel-drive vehicles parked by people in waxed jackets and green wellingtons, the skipper of the *Vital Spark* would not see many changes in the town if he returned today. The wide main street, with family grocers and ironmongers and fishing-tackle shops, seems to qualify for a time capsule.

THOMAS TELFORD AGAIN

Lochgilphead is our gateway for some classic detours. We can drive the nine miles to Crinan, or leave the car and walk the canal towpath. John Rennie started work on the Crinan Canal in 1793; his resident engineer had no experience of canals and four years after it opened the banks burst and it was closed for repair. Repairs lasted just five years: it was closed again in 1811. Thomas Telford was called in to troubleshoot: he rebuilt the canal floor and some of the fifteen locks and the leakproof canal opened for good in 1817.

This short-cut from Loch Fyne to the Atlantic is mainly used today by pleasure craft; Crinan is a favourite yacht anchorage. From Crinan look out to sea. Between the islands of Jura and Scarba is the notorious whirlpool of Corryvrechan and you can hear the angry tide race from considerable distance.

There are more excellent sea views from the village of Kilmartin, ten miles north of Lochgilphead on the A816. The area is littered with the relics of ancient civilisations: standing stones, Pictish carvings

INVERARAY JAILS, old and new: now a major visitor centre with guides dressed as prisoners and warders.

KILMARTIN: Argyll is rich in sculptured stones.

and sculpted gravestones. Kilmartin church has a good collection.

MULL OF McCARTNEY

In contrast to the popularity of the song, the long peninsular Mull of Kintyre is largely neglected by tourists. The Celts called it Dalriada and at Tarbert the Viking chief Magnus the Barefoot, having been promised all the land he could sail round, had his galley dragged across the one-mile isthmus as he stood at the helm. (The name Tarbert may be a corruption of *tarruing*, to draw, and *buta*, a boat.)

From Tarbert a ferry runs to Islay – where Bowmore, Laphroaig and Lagavulin are music to the whisky connoisseur's ears – and to Jura. From Tayinloan, south of Tarbert, we can take the ferry to the little island of Gigha and visit the gardens at Achamore House. The late Sir James Horlock transferred the contents from his garden at Ascot to Achamore lock, stock and begonia.

Campbeltown grew from a castle built in 1609 by the 7th Earl of Argyll. Archibald the Grim, as he was known, also founded the town's whisky industry. Campbeltown has a perfect natural harbour and in the era of sailing ships traded in tobacco, rum and timber with Virginia, the West Indies and the Baltic. Flora Macdonald, saviour of Bonnie Prince Charlie, emigrated to America from Campbeltown with her family.

As the sailing ships have gone, so have the *Chevalier, Princess, Argyll* and *Atlantic*. The locomotives of the Campbeltown to Machrihanish Light Railway, the only narrow-gauge passenger railway in Scotland, made their last journeys in 1932, victims of the economic uncertainties of the times.

8

DUNDEE TO ABERDEEN, A92

Frae Fife, across the silv'ry Tay
Lies Bonnie Dundee, famed for J, J and J.
This once-great seaport, now sadly in decline
Was home to Scotland's best worst poet, whose
verse so rarely scanned or rhymed.

Perhaps before long someone will open a museum in memory of William McGonagall, a wonderful man who modestly wrote: 'Dame Fortune has been

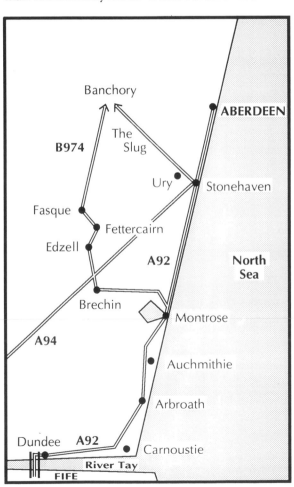

very kind to me by endowing me with the genius of poetry.'

The three Js, a mnemonic impressed on every Scottish schoolchild, are jute, jam and journalism. Jute's halcyon days are over. Down in the docks the main attraction is two floating maritime museums: the forty-six-gun wooden frigate *Unicorn*, the oldest British warship afloat, and the Royal Research Ship *Discovery*, launched in Dundee in 1901 and the ship in which Scott explored the Antarctic.

The Carse of Gowrie, surrounding Dundee and Blairgowrie, is a famous soft-fruit growing area. Jam is still a vital industry but it is marmalade which is in the record-books. It was invented in 1797 by the wife of a Dundee merchant, James Keiller, and the city has the largest, most modern factory in the world.

Journalism means D. C. Thomson, printers and publishers, who publish a variety of newspapers and downmarket magazines. A Dundee institution, the family firm is run on paternalistic Victorian lines – trade unions being considered a counter-productive modern fad – but there are journalists the world over who received their comprehensive, if autocratic, training at Thomson's.

They also publish children's comics. John Cleese described the *Dandy* and the *Beano* as 'the only trustworthy journals in the United Kingdom'. *Dandy* first appeared in 1937 and the *Beano* a year later; through the war years they were strong propagandists with cartoon strips of 'Musso', 'Addie' and 'Hermie' – Mussolini, Hitler and Goering. (The arrival of fiftieth-birthday congratulations from Downing Street prompted cynics to see a link between the former Prime Minister and her cabinet, and the *Beano* strip featuring Teacher and the unruly Bash Street Kids.) More recently, a strip dropped by *Dandy* some years ago – 'Black Bob, the faithful border collie' – has been resurrected in parody by the scurrilous *Viz* comic as 'Black Bag, the faithful border binliner'.

Dundee has little to offer architecturally. Planners of the 1960s completed the destruction of anything of significance that was not vandalised by King Henry VIII. The 'city of discovery' still awaits the initiative – and money – which has gone into cities like Glasgow. St Mary's Tower, Dudhope Castle and Gardyne's House are the oldest surviving buildings; the last is mostly derelict but plans are afoot to renovate it and turn the upper four storeys into an arts and crafts centre. The baroque folly of the Art Gallery's curving staircase is set incongruously amid shopping centres built in the post-modernist concrete slab style, and the Olivetti building is said to look from the air like a giant typewriter.

If you venture uptown to the suburbs – the city centre is down by the river and harbour – you will see a classic *faux-pas* of town planning. The broad streets of the grey suburban housing so common in Scotland have a fifty-yard green belt running up their middles. But the green belt is occupied, as far as the eye can see, by massive pylons carrying electricity cables. The effect is bizarre.

CLAYPOTTS, CARNOUSTIE AND THE COSTA ROSA

As we leave town on the coast road we pass Claypotts Castle. No queues here: the medieval Z-plan tower house, once the home of Graham of Claverhouse (Bonnie Dundee), attracts barely a couple of thousand visitors a year. If it were sited in Edinburgh's Royal Mile it would surely attract millions. The town of Carnoustie is another quiet backwater, despite having a famous golf course. It also has a famous golfing shop, with a roof in the style of a golf umbrella.

Our classic route to Aberdeen is the A92 coast road: those in a hurry will take the inland A94, much of which is dual-carriageway. But we are going to linger along a coastline which if it were in Italy would

be called the Costa Rosa, or in certain lights Sunset Strip. The sandstone stratum, a band running north-south across the Angus shore, the tip of Fife and the middle of East Lothian, crops out in the red rocks and crisp red sands of Lunan Bay and the caves and pinnacles of Red Head near Inverkeillor, and frames the 'Round O' of Arbroath Abbey.

In ancient times the monks kept lanterns burning in that sea-facing oriel window for the benefit of mariners. Long before lighthouses were thought of, the illumination served for a leading mark past the Bell Rock, twelve miles offshore.

THE STONE OF DESTINY

Arbroath has a symbolic place in nationalist politics. Copies of the Declaration of Arbroath are on sale at town stationers and to Scots with a partial view of history it is a sacred document, the definitive word on nationhood. Like the Defenestration of Prague and similar clichés of the history exams it was rather a non-event. Far from being a treaty or agreement, it was merely a letter written by Abbot Linton to the Pope, setting out Scotland's aspirations to have Robert Bruce recognised as king.

Until recently, the Declaration was celebrated with an annual pageant on the abbey lawns. Like St Serf wrestling with the Devil, all the savagery was on one side, all the saintliness on the other. Much was made of English barbarity and the execution of William Wallace in the time-honoured ritual for traitors. The popular contemporary camp-fire entertainment of the Scottish armies – pairing off their captives, stitching their penises together and letting them tear themselves apart – was not portrayed. Parties of schoolchildren attended these performances, soaking up the tactless chauvinism and strident xenophobia. Small wonder if, a few years on, some of them should swell the ranks of the minority of Scots who are the despair of more enlightened nations.

Extremists insist that when the millennium arrives and Scotland achieves her independence the capital city must be Arbroath. The students who burgled Westminster Abbey and removed the Stone of Destiny brought it here. This Stone has inspired a mythology all its own. There are half a dozen

VICTORIA DOCK, DUNDEE: the frigate *Unicorn* and the Antarctic research ship *Discovery* are floating maritime museums.

CLAYPOTTS: medieval tower house was once the home of Graham of Claverhouse, 'Bonnie Dundee'.

AUCHMITHIE: sandstone cliffs above ancient harbour, the 'Musselcrag' of Scott's *The Antiquary*.

CARNOUSTIE: famous golf shop beside a famous golf course.

'authentic' Stones, lodged in various Scottish castles; split into fragments and distributed to patriots; in the safekeeping of the Knights Templar, or maybe the Freemasons; built into the wall of a Glasgow council house . . . to this day newspaper editors with space to fill will send a young reporter off to find the 'real' Stone.

MUSSELCRAG AND MONTROSE

For a short detour to the coast, Auchmithie is a tiny place of great character. The model for Musselcrag in Scott's *The Antiquary* is one of the oldest fishing settlements on the Angus coast. A pebbly track leads from the cliff-top village to the modern harbour, built in the 1890s as part of the herring boom; the days when a fisherman's wages included two bottles of whisky. Spectacular cliffs around Auchmithie have names like De'il's Head, Needle's E'e and Mermaid's Kirk.

We enter Montrose by way of a concrete lookalike suspension bridge, a piece of jokey art-deco. It spans the sea channel at the south end of the River Esk, no longer the torrent of the Angus glens but a broad ribbon of liquid mud draining off the flats of the Basin, or inland sea, of Montrose. What will become of this inland sea? If it were in England it would be a great watersports centre. At present it is a bone of contention between conservationists who want to encourage wildfowl and sporting Montrosians who, following a cherished tradition, want to shoot them.

The town is built on a sandstone ridge which separates the Basin from the sea. By-laws of 1684 specified sandstone as the sole building material. Ninety years later, Boswell and Johnson lodged at the Ship Inn off the High Street, the doctor impressed with the town's neatness. Big Peter, a bell, sounds the curfew at ten in the evening. You are reminded of a Georgian market-town in pink and beige whose era of importance is long past.

When they opened up the main street, rows of gabled cottages were revealed, end on to the street. Strangely, these gable ends offended Scottish notions of architectural propriety and few survive, but players of Montrose football team are nicknamed 'gable-endies'. The docks are no longer stacked with flax

from St Petersburg , tar from Stockholm and oranges from Lisbon. Oil is the big business today: we are less than an hour's drive from Aberdeen. The assets of Montrose harbour board were just £4000 when the board borrowed £4 million from the government to build the oil rig supply base. The money was repaid in record time.

FASQUE AND FETTERCAIRN

Before we continue up the coast road to Aberdeen, there is an agreeable detour inland through the Mearns country. Nine miles from Montrose lies Brechin, the birthplace of Sir Robert Watson-Watt who invented radar. The cathedral has a round tower of Celtic origin, probably a monks' refuge from maurauding Vikings. Older still are the standing stones with Pictish carvings at Aberlemno, between Brechin and Forfar.

We can take the B966 through a sylvan landscape past the walled heraldic gardens of Edzell, whose creation all but bankrupted Sir David Lindsay in the early seventeenth century; past the whitewashed buildings of Scotland's second oldest distillery at Fettercairn; through the Fettercairn Arch, built to commemorate the visit of Queen Victoria in 1861; and on to Fasque, where Victoria's prime minister Gladstone had his Scottish retreat.

Set in deer parkland, the baronial house offers a glimpse of 'upstairs, downstairs' life: the kitchens and servants' quarters are perfectly preserved, with handwritten signs adding to the charm of a charming house. Northbound to Banchory, the B974 is a well-surfaced and little-used road which takes in some classic scenery.

STONEHAVEN, STOKER
AND THE SLUG

The ruins of Dunnottar Castle tower above Stonehaven. William Wallace took it from the English in 1296 and torched it, roasting the inhabitants alive. Four centuries later in the 'Killing Times', 167 Covenanters were suffocated and starved to death in the dungeons. The cliff-top ruin with its grisly history is a great favourite with film-makers.

(Slains, another castle on this coastline, north of Aberdeen, inspired the young Bram Stoker to write a story about a certain vampire bat.)

Stonehaven with its double harbour is the archetypal Scottish fishing town. Wynds and pends slope off the main street to a seafront which comes right up to the houses. Out of this weekend haunt of Aberdonian anglers, all roads lead up. The wide A94 swallows up our little A92. Another A-road, known by the unenticing name of the Slug, provides a scenic short-cut to Deeside.

Off the Slug, the purlieus of Ury have been put forward as the possible battle site of Mons Graupius, where Agricola defeated the Picts in AD 84. Curiously, considering that in terms of numbers involved this was the greatest battle ever fought on British soil, no one has been able to fix even its approximate location.

9

DUNDEE TO BRAEMAR

*I was tempit at Pittempton, Draiglet at
Baldragon,
Striken at Strike martin, And Killed at
Martinstane.*

Not McGonagall, but the dying declaration of the dragon of Strathmartine, who devoured nine maidens at Nine Maidens' Well and paid the price at

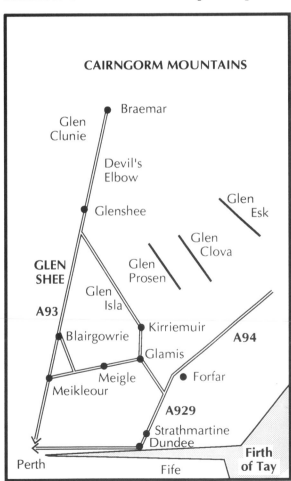

the hands of Martin, bereaved lover of one of the girls. The 1793 *Statistical Account of Scotland* adds puritanically that 'the girls were all sisters who had gone out on a Sunday evening to fetch water' . . . implying that by breaking the Sabbath they deserved their fate. Heading north out of Dundee on the A929 Glamis road, we pass close to Strathmartine, now on the edge of the city suburbs. Though the church dedicated to St Martin in 1249 was demolished in 1799, there are still a number of curious carved stones in the churchyard.

Six miles from Dundee we leave the dual-carriageway and cross the A94 towards Glamis. The history of Scotland's most haunted castle goes back ten centuries. The intention was to build it on nearby Hunter's Hill, but when the masons arrived each morning they found the stonework dismantled by unseen hands and moved to the valley below. Eventually they took the hint.

Glamis has endless royal connections. King Malcolm II is believed to have died there in 1034 when it was the hunting lodge of the Scottish kings. Macbeth, Thane of Glamis, James V and Queen Elizabeth, the Queen Mother, were all residents. Mary, Queen of Scots stayed on her way to Huntly Castle and Randolph, the English 'ambassador' (spy) reported to Queen Elizabeth I: 'despite extreme Fowle and Colde weather I never saw her merrier, never dismayed'.

Less tangible residents include a Grey Lady in the chapel; the Glamis Monster, confined to a secret room which ghostbusters have been unable to locate (you can see a window outside for which there is no

MEIGLE STONE NO. 4: Tayside is rich in sculptured stones; there are twenty-five in the school at Meigle.

corresponding inner room); a madman on the roof; a Lady of Glamis, burned at the stake for witchcraft; and Earl Beardie, who has spent the last 500 years playing dice with the Devil for his soul. You may feel safer in the grounds, laid out by Capability Brown. The twenty-one-foot sundial has eighty-four dials.

FROM BEARDIE TO BARRIE

We have a choice of routes going north. The quieter road goes through Kirriemuir and Glen Isla. James Matthew Barrie was born at 9 Brechin Road, Kirriemuir in 1860 and his birthplace museum, in the care of the National Trust for Scotland, includes the outside wash-house which was the playwright's first theatre. A philanthropist, Barrie donated a portion of his royalties from *Peter Pan* to London's Great Ormond Street Hospital (for children), and made similar provisions in his will.

The southern slopes of the Grampian mountains are pierced by deep glens: Esk, Clova, Prosen and Isla. The first three are dead-ends; a drive of twenty miles or more ending at some grand Victorian hunting lodge, for the moors are alive with the call of the grouse. The B951 follows the fourth through Glen Isla, scenic in summer and bleak in winter, meeting the A93 just south of the Spittal of Glenshee.

MEIGLE AND MEIKLEOUR

The longer way to Glenshee is the A94 to Coupar Angus and on to the A93 at Blairgowrie. There are Pictish and standing stones dotted all over Tayside: you can see a collection of twenty-five at Meigle, housed in the former school to arrest weathering. For another curiosity, it is worth taking two short sides of a triangle to visit Meikleour. The mile-long beech hedge, the tallest in Britain, is said to have been planted by men who went to fight for Bonnie Prince Charlie at Culloden, and never came home.

North of Edinburgh and Glasgow, Scotland is not noted for busy roads, particularly in winter. The A93 can be an exception. From first light cars may be on the move, roof-racks laden with skis, for of the country's five ski centres Glenshee is the closest to Edinburgh. Twenty runs are spread across the slopes of Glas Maol, Meall Odhar, Cairnwell and Cairn

Aosda: all over 3000 feet. Scotland has several hundred mountains of this height or more, known as 'Munros' after mountaineer Sir Hugh Munro who first categorised them.

THE WHITE SPORT

Only the most incompetent stockbroker would advise you to invest in a Scottish ski company. Recent mild winters have brought the industry in places close to bankruptcy. Serious skiers make for the Alps where the weather is more predictable or take advantage of cheap packages in eastern Europe. Moreover, conservationists fronted by the Royal Society for the Protection of Birds habitually castigate the 'booming leisure industry which seeks to turn remote valleys into ski resorts' and allege that ptarmigan, snow bunting, raven and golden eagle are victims of farming, forestry and the ski industry. In the late 1980s Lurcher's Gully, an inaccessible area of the Cairngorms earmarked for ski-development expansion, was rarely out of the letters' columns of the Scottish press.

Across the country in Lochaber, the opening of Scotland's latest ski centre at Aonach Mor after ten years of planning controversy was almost a disaster. At the launch a cable snapped and two dozen journalists and PR people were stranded in the restaurant halfway up the mountain: a gruelling experience.

GATHERING OF THE CLANS

Over the Devil's Elbow we cross the regional boundary into Grampian and follow the Clunie Water down to Braemar. At an altitude of 1100 feet and fifty miles from the sea, the town in winter frequently records the lowest temperatures in Britain. Even in summer there is a sudden chill when the sun goes down. The turreted castle a mile to the east was built in 1628 by the Earl of Mar, and a later earl, on a site now occupied by a hotel, raised the standard of the Old Pretender in the 1715 Jacobite uprising. In 1881 Robert Louis Stevenson stayed at The Cottage in Braemar and wrote most of *Treasure Island*. Annually Braemar hosts the largest of the Highland Gatherings and in the first week of September the population swells to 20,000.

The Duffs and the Farquharsons, the Forbes and the Grants . . . in ancient times the Gathering was a simple assembly of those north-eastern clans, an opportunity for the clansmen to see and be seen by their chiefs, to present weapons for inspection and discuss problems and, for diversion, to engage in some competitive wrestling, running and dancing.

The picturesque events of the modern Games are traced to picturesque origins. Sword dancing is supposed to have evolved in the eleventh century, when King Malcolm overcame a chief of the Macbeths and, crossing the swords of victor and vanquished, danced a jig over them. The reels and flings are believed to have been inspired by the mating rituals of the red deer. Mountain racing – to the top of a hill and back – was first included in the Games at the request of a medieval monarch dissatisfied with the poor performance of the royal messengers.

Today, tourist propaganda and the mobility of modern transport have transformed Highland Gatherings into orgiastic occasions. You pay £2 to park your car in a swamp and £10 to have a tractor pull it out. The hammer-throwing, shot-putting and caber-tossing are subsidiary to the main event of the day, which is to see who can get drunk fastest. The general standard of behaviour, if seen at an open-air rock concert, would make headlines in the press and bring calls for such events to be banned.

THE KILT AND TARTANITIS

Braemar and tartan are inseparable. But Sir John Sinclair and others have pointed out that an Englishman invented the kilt. The bagpipes too are a foreign invention. No matter. Scots have been occupied with inventing everything from television to the telephone, the bicycle, rubber tyres, steam power, the adhesive postage stamp . . . we can safely leave the trivia of the kilt and the bagpipes to lesser nations.

As we travel Scotland, a man in a kilt is a sight to stop and stare at. The tartan tie and 'bunnet' (cap) are the prerogative of visiting Americans. Highlandmen who attend a Gathering will wear the kilt for old times' sake – it may well be the kilt their grandfathers wore – and an older generation of Scotsmen consider it the correct dress for weddings and formal occasions. Even Lowlanders concede that wearing the kilt makes you feel six inches taller.

The original garment was a length of woollen cloth measuring six feet by fifteen feet: a camouflaged travelling tent. After Culloden, the British government proscribed it. A first offence carried a six-month sentence and a second offence seven years' transportation to the Colonies. The law was repealed in 1782 and when King George IV made his state visit to Edinburgh in 1822 he wore a kilt. The disease we diagnose today as tartanitis is attributable in part to George IV, Queen Victoria, Prince Albert and Sir Walter Scott.

The kilt *can* look good, accompanied by sporran, brogue shoes and a dark or tweed jacket, especially if the tartan is a sober one. But the pattern lends itself to endless variation and in recent times companies, golf clubs and tourist organisations have had their own designer tartans woven. Glasgow Rangers football club has its own tartan, a particularly unsubtle one, as do the American sailors at Holy Loch who sport their Polaris tartan. The cult has further intensified as hotel chains have introduced targes, claymores, antlers and wall-to-wall tartan carpeting and wallpaper in their cocktail bars. (If you are still determined to find your family tartan, the Clan Tartan Centre, Bangor Road, Leith, Edinburgh, has a computer database and will give you a print-out of your clan history, if a connection exists.)

Braemar is the end of our route, for here the Clunie flows into the Dee, and our royal route through Deeside is described in Chapter 15. Sensitive souls will not wish to stay in Braemar where hotels vary between the seedy and the overpriced, but will continue on to the more dignified Ballater or Aboyne.

MEIKLEOUR: tallest beech hedge in Britain, planted by men who went to fight at Culloden and never came home.

GLENSHEE: recent mild winters have put Scotland's ski industries on the edge of bankruptcy.

10

PERTH TO OBAN, A85

Scotland has many coastal routes, but few which link coast to coast. The A85 from Dundee to Oban is a classic. In a hundred miles you swap the North Sea off the east coast for the Atlantic Ocean off the west. You leave the cultivated Perthshire farmlands, cross the Highland Line, and discover Argyll's majestic mountains. Topography, architecture, accents all change in a short drive.

We pick up the A85 westbound from Perth

and, travelling parallel to the River Almond, pass a famous castle: Huntingtower. Mary, Queen of Scots spent her second honeymoon here and in those days it was known as Ruthven Castle – until James VI proscribed the name of the family who kidnapped him.

It is only a short distance to Crieff, past neat little fields and windbreak patches of woodland. The fields in May are fluorescent yellow with oilseed rape

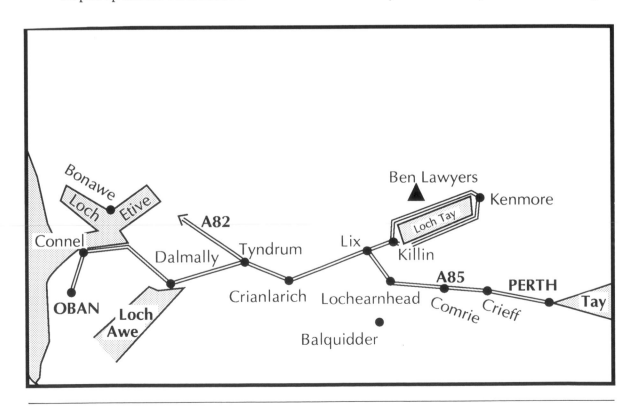

HUNTINGTOWER: the castle has fine painted ceilings and was the scene of a royal kidnap.

OILSEED RAPE: good for farmers' bank balances; misery for asthma sufferers.

flowers and as we leave Tayside we recall a recent book on the region by Evelyn Hood, in which she praises the local farmers for their innovation and adaptability in planting this crop. She appears to have got it spectacularly wrong. This evil weed, whose main benefit is to boost the bank balances of farmers, a cash crop proliferating all over Britain, is a source of misery for asthma sufferers.

Its pollen is so heavy it has created a new intake. Study programmes started recently at Dundee and Aberdeen Universities have produced initially some interesting statistics. About forty per cent of the population is allergic to oilseed rape pollen; researchers allow a control figure – the number of people allergic to any kind of pollen – of six or seven per cent. There are reports from beekeepers too, of oily and inedible honey.

THE SAN FRANCISCO OF SCOTLAND

The Highland Line, which crosses Scotland diagonally from Stonehaven to Rothesay, is an economic, geological and geographical line which separates the Highlands from the Lowlands. (In its economic role it is flexible, having moved four hundred miles south to become the north/south divide. Currently it crosses from the Wash to the Bristol Channel.) The villages of Crieff and Comrie sit on a fault on the geological Highland Line, and the inhabitants occasionally experience mild earth tremors.

Crieff in summer crawls with coach parties. The town takes tourism very seriously and shops sell Scottish passports, haggis eggs and rubber Loch Ness Monsters. At the last count there were four visitor centres, where the promise of a seconds shop and a factory tour is sufficient to lure the tourist into the complex.

Glenturret Distillery is in the *Guinness Book of Records*, not because of its claim to be the oldest in the country – half a dozen contest this title – but because of Towser. Cats are attracted to the warmth of still-rooms and by tradition are encouraged since rodents are attracted to grain stores. Long-haired tortoiseshell Towser notched up 28,899 rats and mice before she died in 1987, a month short of her twenty-

fourth birthday. Perhaps her longevity was due to inhaling the spirit fumes, for on the subject of whisky James Hogg wrote: 'If a body could find oot the exac' proper proportion and quantity that ought to be drunk every day, and keep to that, I verily trow that he might leeve forever, withoot dying at a', and that doctors and kirkyairds would go oot o' fashion.'

ROB ROY, ROMANS AND A ROCK GARDEN

Comrie, seven miles west, is a similar version of Crieff: all gift and antique shops. From St Fillans with its riverside picnic areas the road hugs the loch into Lochearnhead, with a watersports centre and a cluster of Bed and Breakfasts (B&B). South are the Trossachs and a step away on trout- and salmon-rich Loch Voil is Balquhidder. The red-haired extortionist Rob Roy is buried in the churchyard along with some of his gang, the 'children of the mist'.

North through Glen Ogle we climb more than 1000 feet and descend rapidly to the Lix Toll. The fifty-ninth (LIX) Roman Legion was stationed here. Our route continues west through Glen Dochart but we might detour through Killin and along Loch Tay. The Falls of Dochart at Killin – where a stone arch bridges crystal-clear water tumbling over mossy boulders – for many visitors epitomise the Highlands. Or perhaps the glut of caravan sites is the overwhelming impression the visitor takes home.

The single-track road signposted Ardeonaig and skirting the south side of Loch Tay is a better bet than the main road to the north. You are better placed to appreciate the size of Ben Lawers reflected in the water. The visitor centre near its summit has a contentious history and represents an uneasy compromise. Environmentalists in the 1930s scotched plans for a ski development, prophesying damage to the rare alpine plants. Then in 1950 the National Trust for Scotland bought the 'largest and finest rock garden in the country', a Grade One site of scientific interest, and built their mountain visitor centre. But just how you protect and preserve rare plants and wildlife by encouraging trippers *en masse* to trample all over their unique habitat is a mystery. The skiers finally got their way too: the Scottish Ski Club has a base at Coire Odhar.

Passing Croft na Caber, a new watersports centre, we reach the end of Loch Tay at Kenmore. The village was built by the Marquess of Breadalbane in the nineteenth century and boasts a venerable hotel. Queen Victoria was amused here in 1842 with fireworks and a procession of barges. In recent times the annual highlight is the Kenmore to Aberfeldy raft-race, when local pub teams compete in a no-holds-barred contest by day and a no-expense-spared drinking contest by night.

Westbound from Crianlarich, five miles of Strathfillan to Tyndrum forms a unique valley, the only one in Britain to have two main railway lines, from Glasgow to Oban and to Fort William. Since hostelries in the Highlands tend to belong in one of two categories – spartan or tartan – it is worth a short detour down Glen Falloch to the Drovers (officially the Inverinan Arms). Amid Victorian furnishings, the clientele are mostly kagoul-clad backpackers, for we are close to a long-distance footpath, the West Highland Way.

THE HOLLOW MOUNTAIN

From Tyndrum the A82 climbs towards Glencoe. Our route sweeps west down Glen Lochy to Dalmally, hurrying to reach the sea. Kilchurn Castle, high on the list of Scotland's top ten scenic ruins, sits brooding on the shores of Loch Awe. Seen shrouded in early-morning mist it evokes turbulent history and the days when fierce Highlanders fought over the few fertile glens in this untamed, mountainous terrain.

The Falls of Cruachan have been tamed and the mountain is hollow. Inside Ben Cruachan electric buses ferry you through the North of Scotland Hydro Board's storage pumping station, where surplus electricity is used to pump water from Loch Awe up to Loch Cruachan. Emerging, blinking, into the sunlight from this hall of the mountain king, you can detect the tang of the sea, which grows stronger as you continue down the Pass of Brander, a narrow defile squeezed between mountain and loch.

A STOMACH WHICH DEMANDS FEEDING

Our first sight of the sea is Loch Etive. On its shores is the blast-furnace of Bonawe, Scotland's answer to

Coalbrookdale in Shropshire. (Diderot's *Encyclopaedia*, published in 1763, describes a working blast-furnace with indelicate metaphor: like 'a stomach which demands feeding steadily, regularly and endlessly. It is subject to changes in behaviour through lack of nourishment, to indigestion and embarrassing eruptions through too rich or voluminous a diet . . .).'

Abraham Darby used coke for smelting at Coalbrookdale; charcoal was the fuel at Bonawe. Smelters of this type, with water-powered bellows, were common in Scotland in the seventeenth and eighteenth centuries, for the Highlands provided a cheap and abundant supply of wood from the great Caledonian forest. The liquid metal was run off into a mould known as a sow; the connecting moulds were called pigs and hence the term pig-iron.

Bonawe was in operation from 1753 to 1876 and produced, apart from pig-iron, cannonballs fired at the battle of Trafalgar. Iron ore from Cumbria was not the only commodity to arrive in Bonawe Quay for the workforce of six hundred. In 1781 the company's agent called it 'a principal smuggling harbour' and said 'I believe there is not such another drunken hole in the Kingdom.'

GATEWAY TO THE ISLANDS

Past Connel our route skirts the headland and we can see tantalising glimpses of the islands of Kerrera, Lismore and mountainous Mull. The ruins of Dunstaffnage Castle, on a promontory where Loch Etive meets Loch Linnhe, date from the thirteenth century. But there is thought to have been a fort here since the fifth century, for legend has it that the Stone of Destiny, Jacob's pillow on the plains of Luz, came to Dunstaffnage from Ireland, and that the Scottish kings were crowned here until the Stone was taken to Scone, which became the capital of the united Picts and Scots in the ninth century. Dunstaffnage Castle also has connections with Robert Bruce and was a transit prison of Flora Macdonald, on her way to London to answer for aiding and abetting the escape of Bonnie Prince Charlie.

Oban occupies a natural amphitheatre, curving round a bay with the natural protection of the island of Kerrera. There is nothing natural about Oban's

KILCHURN: imposing ruined castle on Loch Awe, a former stronghold of the Clan Campbell.

Bᴏɴᴀᴡᴇ: well-preserved remains of a charcoal-fuelled blast furnace, once a common sight in the Highlands.

infamous landmark, MacCaig's Folly. The incomplete Colosseum lookalike was a local banker's monument to self-esteem – but he went bankrupt.

Down by the harbour, the seagulls are not quite as well-fed as they were twenty years ago. Back then the quays were stacked high with exotic shellfish. In the era of the Scampi Boom, Oban was the clearing-house for the produce of sandy bays and inlets within a fifty-mile radius. Ramshackle vans made their weekly fish-runs from tiny anchorages: Norway lobsters on the first stage of their journey to London restaurants. The government gave generous grants to aspiring fishermen to buy their own boats.

The boom lasted only a few years. In a lucrative but unregulated free-for-all the bays were virtually fished out. Oban survives today on tourism and as a gateway to the islands: the terminus of some twenty-three ferries run by MacBraynes. Oban has a visitor centre, a distillery, a clutch of gift shops and tearooms and, in case you thought punning shop names were

the prerogative of hairdressers, a wholefood shop called Oban Sesame. The Rare Breeds Farm, a recent venture at Barranrioch, is environmentally-sound, and so is the Sea Life centre at Barcaldine.

SEAL WATCH

We might have lost our appetites for visitor centres round about Crieff, near the start of our route, but marine ecologists at Barcaldine are doing valuable research into grey and common seals. Their Seal Watch campaign is prompted by the observation that both species are in decline around Britain's coasts. Recently the distemper virus wiped out many thousands of seals and the current theory is that increasing levels of PCB pollutants may be adversely affecting breeding levels.

For, as the naturalist W. R. Mitchell has pointed out, 'man is the biggest predator of them all'.

11

OBAN TO IONA
BY TOBERMORY

The first stage of our pilgrim's route to Iona is by sea, so we offer up a prayer to those Lords of the Western Isles, Caledonian MacBrayne. CalMac, as they are called, operate the ferry from Oban to Mull.

Oban is not exactly a Dover or a Portsmouth. CalMac's ticket office opens around ten and closes for lunch around ten past. Ask someone wearing a vague resemblance to a uniform the time of the next boat and he will tell you it has just left. These are the Western Isles, where clocks and watches have never really caught on. The visitor must learn that words like 'immediately' and 'hurry' do not form part of the Western Islander's vocabulary.

Some things do change: our boat is new. Though several times larger than its predecessor, it would still fit on the car deck of a cross-channel ferry. When it was launched a couple of years ago someone noticed it was six feet too short for marine safety. In

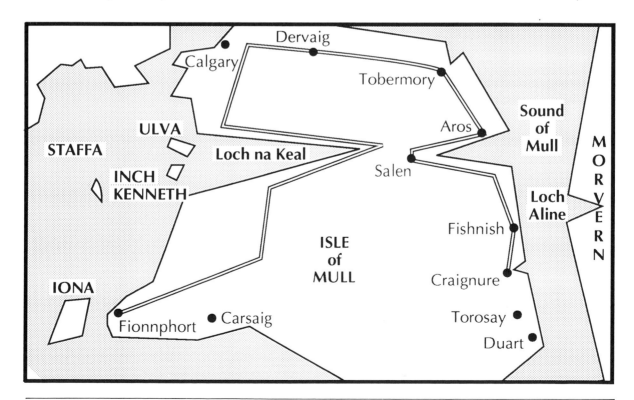

TOBERMORY BAY: a favourite anchorage for west-coast yachtsmen;
the colour-washed buildings on the seafront form a famous facade.

LOCH SUNART: looking towards the Atlantic, with Morvern to the south and Ardnamurchan to the north.

due course it came out of service, went into dry dock, was cut in half, and had a six-foot section welded in.

The old boat had more character. It had a tiny oak-panelled lounge where, during the forty-five minute journey, you could hide from maurauding gangs of seagulls up on deck. You embarked by way of a dilapidated iron ramp and the car deck was so miniscule they used an iron turntable and brute force to pack in cars and trucks like sardines. The writers of *You Have Been Warned*, a 1930s Highway Code parody, must have travelled the Oban-Mull ferry: 'Question: why does a car ferry always carry a staff of two? Answer: one to say ''stop'' while the other says ''come on''.'

As you enter the Sound of Mull, the deepwater channel between the island and Morvern, a famous landmark comes into view. Duart Castle has been guarding the entrance to the sound for seven centuries and, except for a brief period, the Macleans have been in residence since 1390. In 1745 Sir Hector Maclean, a Stuart sympathiser, found himself on the losing side: he was sent to the Tower of London and the estate was forfeited. The castle was recovered in 1911 and restored by his descendants. Its attractions include the cells where officers from the Spanish galleon wrecked in Tobermory Bay were incarcerated, and an exhibition on the Scout movement.

WORTH ITS WEIGHT IN BUTTER

On a clear day, as the ferry turns into Craignure Bay another castle is visible to the north, on the mainland by Loch Aline. Tradition has it that Kinlochaline Tower was built by an Amazon of the Clan McInnes, who paid the architect with its volume in butter. A third coastal fortress is Torosay, whose gardens contain a famous Italian statue walk. In summer a narrow-gauge railway runs a mile and a half through some impressive scenery from Craignure pier to Torosay.

FISHNISH TO MISHNISH

Going north on the A849 – a motorway in comparison with the rest of our route – we pass close to Fishnish, where a tiny ferry crosses to the hamlet of Lochaline on Morvern. (The sands of Loch Aline are said to be the purest in Europe: they supply raw

material for the makers of crystal and optical lenses.) We pass Mull's aerodrome by the Glenforza hotel and, where the road divides at Salen, continue towards Tobermory (Well of St Mary), or 'Tob' as Muilleachs abbreviate their capital. Aros Castle is now a ruin: in olden days it was a base of the Lords of the Isles who extracted a toll from passing shipping.

A tunnel of rhododendrons leads into Tobermory, a half-size replica of Oban. The architecture is less random than Oban's, with a fine row of brightly-painted houses, including the legendary Mishnish hotel, along the seafront, including the legendary Mishnish hotel, along the seafront. Built two hundred years ago as a major fishing port, Tobermory never lived up to its founders' expectations, but today is treasured by anglers and yachtsmen as one of the best-sheltered havens on the west coast.

The Spanish galleon in Tobermory Bay is the subject of periodic salvage operations. In 1588 Donald Glas MacLean, a hostage on board *San Juan de Sicilia*, set fire to the magazine. Despite rumours of massive hoards of Spanish gold, only a few trinkets have been found to date.

QUINISH, MORNISH AND TRESHNISH

As you climb through peaty moorland on the Dervaig road, look north over Mull's promontory of Quinish. On a clear day you can see Ardnamurchan, the most westerly point of mainland Britain, with a lighthouse whose lamp still revolves by clockwork. In the former Free Church manse outside Dervaig is Mull Little Theatre, a possible contender for the *Guinness Book of Records*. It has thirty-seven seats and the stage is so small that when the current production requires a cast of more than three the extras have to be played as puppets. The theatre has become an institution: seats are reserved from across the Atlantic.

Leaving Dervaig we come to the Old Byre, since we have not managed to leave those ubiquitous heritage centres behind us on the mainland. The museum of community history depicts the crofters' lifestyle at the time of the Highland Clearances. It was an emigrant from the next hamlet, Calgary, who founded the Canadian city. On a sunny day nowhere seems to have such white sands and such blue sea as Calgary Bay. Turning south, we see in a couple of miles a track on the right: it leads to the deserted village of Crakaig Treshnish where chimneys cut into the caves suggest the production of illicit whisky in days gone by.

LORD ULLIN'S DAUGHTER

Scotland has around 750 islands. We are within easy sailing distance of half of them, and within sight of some famous ones as Loch na Keal forces us inland. The lake cuts a deep bite out of Mull and is a favourite haunt of seals and sharks (the harmless basking variety); it is also the 'dark Loch Gyle' of Thomas Campbell's ballad:

> *Now who be ye would cross Loch Gyle,*
> *This dark and stormy water?*
> *Oh, I'm the chief of Ulva's Isle,*
> *And this Lord Ullin's daughter.*

Past Ulva, with its little offshoot Gometra – like a ewe with a lamb – we come round the south side of Loch na Keal on a road which squeezes dramatically between cliff and sea . . . until the road gives up the struggle and turns inland. Ahead of us: Ben More (3169 ft), Mull's highest mountain – an easy climb, but beware the headless horseman! Behind us: Inch Kenneth, the island which Johnson and Boswell visited in 1773. 'The most agreeable Sunday I ever passed,' wrote the doctor, though he described Mull generally as 'a most dolorous country'.

SURPASSES THE FINEST CATHEDRAL

Eight miles out in the Atlantic lies the geological freak of Staffa. This stupendous basaltic grotto was unknown to the outside world until 1772, when the naturalist Sir Joseph Banks ran aground on the island on his way to Iceland.

The chief attraction is Fingal's Cave – the name in Gaelic, *Uaimh Binn*, means musical cave – which inspired Mendelssohn's overture and John Keats to write 'for solemnity and grandeur it far surpasses the finest cathedral'. There are other caves, columns and pillars. Until recently the only way to get to Staffa was to haggle with local off-duty fishermen. Now several

organisations run summer trips, the favoured departure point being Fionnphort on the south-west tip of Mull. Choose a calm day: landing facilities are rudimentary, with slippery rocks and often a heavy Atlantic swell.

Before we reach Fionnphort there are two other natural curiosities to look at. From Balneanach Farm a footpath leads down to Mackinnon's Cave, a cavern so vast that legend says it stretches right across Mull. Access is at low tide only. Fingal's Table, the stone inside the entrance, may be an early Christian altar. Low tide is also the time to visit Carsaig Arches (take the single-track road to Carsaig from Pennyghael, off the A849). A three-mile walk along the coast leads to these tunnels carved by the sea out of basaltic rock. *En route* you pass the Nuns' Cave, supposed to have provided shelter for nuns driven from Iona during the Reformation.

THE SACRED ISLE

Like Carsaig Arches, you will have to visit Iona on foot too: visitors' cars are not allowed. Getting there in winter is not always possible, as the tide rips through the narrow straight between Fionnphort and the Iona jetty and the little ferry bobs around like a frenzied cork. But in summer, when the quartzite rock sparkles in the sun and the sea shimmers deep, deep blue as it washes the brilliant sands . . . you can see why St Columba chose Iona for his monastery in AD 563.

'We were now treading that illustrious Island which was once the luminary of the Caledonian regions . . . ' begins one of Dr Johnson's most celebrated passages of sonorous prose. Here we have the burial ground of the Scottish kings (between twenty and thirty; opinions vary) including Macbeth, at Reilig Odhrain, the 'Westminster Abbey of Scotland'. Columba's original monastery, frequently attacked by Norse raiders; was replaced in 1203 and there are five elaborately-carved high crosses which date from between the eighth and tenth centuries. The careful and thorough restoration work was largely the inspiration of the Very Reverend Dr George Macleod, Lord Macleod of Fuinary, who founded the Iona Community in 1938.

We have taken the long way round Mull to the

Sacred Isle. Despite recent signs of the yuppies moving in, for you can buy a farm on Mull from the proceeds of a one-bedroom flat in London, Mull has a unique atmosphere and you need time to let the wonderful untamed scenery work its magic on you.

According to an ancient prophesy, Iona would seem the place to be when the end of the world comes, in a 'watery deluge':

> *While, with the great and good,*
> *Columba's happy isle shall rear*
> *Her towers above the flood.*

12

TYNDRUM TO INVERNESS, A82

Far to the east, Loch Tummel; just ahead, Rannoch Moor; in the distance, Lochaber . . . as far as Fort William our classic route is the Road to the Isles, the one authenticated in the song. We leave behind us birch- and pine-clad rolling slopes of northern Perthshire, exchanging them for a primordial landscape of mountain and peat bog, a landscape unchanged since dinosaur days. Fish trucks, returning empty to west Highland harbours, make

the steady climb across Black Mount with ease before the descent into Glencoe.

Travel books and guide books encourage us to shiver as the high crags close in. The name, we are told, means 'Glen of Weeping', although that etymology is suspect. The temperature plummets, they say, even on the hottest day. The corridor through the hills is a gloomy defile, the route suffused with memories of shame and disaster, the

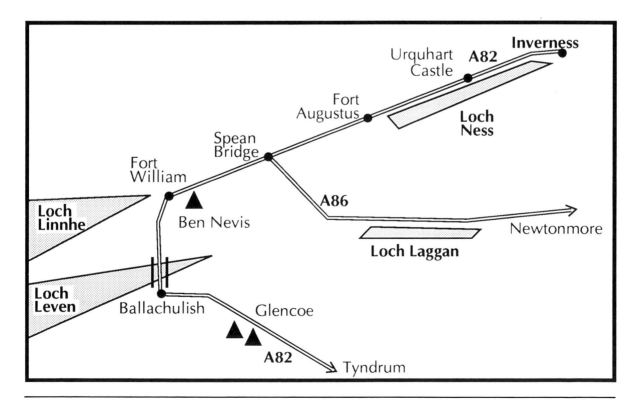

GLENCOE: the order for the massacre was said to have been written on the back of a playing-card, the nine of diamonds, known as 'the curse of Scotland'.

ghosts of clan tragedies hover over your roof-rack.

If your name is Macdonald you are entitled to shiver. By those scree slopes and up those rivulets which cascade into the Coe your ancestors scrambled in panic and February sleet at three in the morning. Under the bridges by which you cross and recross the stream the half-naked women and children cowered for safety, but few escaped the bayonet. On those fearful heights the survivors gathered and saw their huts burning and their cattle – their whole livelihood – driven away.

The massacre of 1692, in which the Campbells paid off old scores against the Macdonalds with interest, was probably not the most brutal or important act of genocide in the history of Highland tribes. Ambush, assault, vendetta and trickery were their way of life. But the Glencoe massacre has most pages in the history books. It involved national politics and is therefore better documented than any other.

Ignorant of those old woes, you would find Glencoe a verdant narrow valley of some grandeur. In winter the heights of Buachaille Etive Mór and its shouldering mountains are brilliantly defined and their slopes are brightened with skiers: this is the winter-sports area nearest to Glasgow. Part of the glen is in NTS hands. Material at the visitor centre tells you all you need to know about the massacre of three centuries back and about the variegated wildlife of the region. The older monuments are in Glencoe village at the foot of the pass.

In more recent bad old days, Glencoe village was where you joined the queue for the Ballachulish ferry, three miles away. Now you cross Loch Leven by a bridge so simple and short you can't understand why it wasn't built a century ago. If you want to know what the ferry was like, its surviving twin still crosses Loch Linnhe at Corran, which we pass *en route* to Fort William. The little raft which crabs its way across to the Ardgour shore gives you the options of a quieter road to Fort William or two peninsular detours to Morvern and Ardnamurchan.

CAPITAL OF THE WEST HIGHLANDS

There are few who are not disappointed with their first taste of Fort William. It does not live up to the promise in its name, nor to its title as capital of the West Highlands. Passengers boarding the overnight Fort William sleeper at London Euston are anxious to know at what hour dawn breaks in those northern latitudes, and whether they will be able to see anything of Rannoch Moor or Ben Nevis. Their first romantic experience could well be stumbling out at a small station whose exit to the town is a concrete tunnel adorned with anti-English graffiti. A one-horse town – but without the horse – Fort William is all souvenir shops and a clutch of pompous-looking hotels, none of them meriting an entry in the guide book. Its redeeming feature is the efficiency of its bypass.

Worse is to come as we continue north. The Great Glen, one of Scotland's premier scenic attractions, announces itself with a spectacle reminiscent of Calcutta or Shanghai: horrid little chalets, cabins, caravans and hencoops jostling for position around the head of Loch Linnhe like the pustules of some dreadful disease. And right in their midst is an engineering triumph which deserves to come into national care, perhaps to be walled off and visited through turnstiles: the Banavie locks, the flight known as Neptune's Staircase, the western end of the Caledonian Canal. Somewhere down by the shore is the house built for Thomas Telford when he came to supervise the building of the canal. But we will not stray into the slums of this anarchic-looking otherworld for fear of getting a knife in our backs.

Behind us now is Ben Nevis, Britain's highest mountain at 4408 feet. Access by a footpath at the head of Glen Nevis is straightforward enough (cars have been driven to the summit), a long unremarkable walk. Or let the cable car take the strain: a gondola (they should have called it a *pendula*) will carry you most of the way up Aonach Mor, Nevis's sister mountain and the site of Scotland's newest ski resort.

TELFORD'S TRIUMPH

Ahead, the Great Glen lives up to its promise. River valleys which broaden into ribbons of lochs, copious streams dashing down from formidable hills, occasional villages of genuine Highland character – fresh white-painted gabled cottages; modest country

AONACH MOR: the gondola, the easy way to the top of Ben Nevis's sister mountain.

shops – and deep cuttings smothered in pinewoods to the water's edge, making the sixty-mile journey to Inverness a landscape adventure.

Ideas for adapting the Great Glen to a coast-to-coast waterway proliferated in the latter half of the eighteenth century. Thomas Telford's proposal, which was accepted, was to cut channels twenty feet deep between the three lochs and their exits to the sea. The estimate was a mere £350,000: mile for mile the cheapest canal on record, because nature had done most of the work.

Digging began in 1804. On paper the technology was straightforward. But the next six years were unusually wet ones, even for the Highlands, and Telford had terrible problems with landslides and running sand and gravel which filled up the channels as fast as they were dug. He had labour problems too. Government hopes that a few years' honest labour at excellent rates of pay ($7\frac{1}{2}$p per day) would tame the savage Hielandman into a law-abiding citizen were not realised. Local lairds made extravagant claims for loss of amenity. Telford built no fewer than seven bridges for one landowner to give his cattle access to the other bank, and then the landowner put in a claim for a loss-of-earnings grant, for time wasted in persuading the cattle to cross.

One eyewitness of the project was James Hogg, returning from a walking tour: 'We came to the embryos of the Caledonian Canal, at which a great number of people were employed . . . the advances they make are not great . . . the labourers were dabbling carelessly with picks and spades . . . looking around them at everything which was to be seen . . . I could not help viewing it as a hopeless job.' Not until 1820 was the grand design realised. The steamboat pioneer Henry Bell immediately put his paddle-steamer *Stirling Castle* on the Fort Augustus-Inverness run.

But times were changing. The Caledonian Canal was intended to give security to shipping in the Napoleonic Wars and to short-cut the hazardous passage round the north of Scotland. By the time it opened there was no prospect of war and the invention of steam had reduced the dangers of coastal voyages. Several locks collapsed. One section or another was always closed for repair.

The canal never showed a profit. Telford died in 1834 believing he had wasted twenty years on a white elephant. He may have agreed with the contemporary who wrote 'Perhaps a prejudiced fellow like me may think that one-third of the money laid out on the Great Canal would have been better employed in buying land for those tribes and families now vomited out, forced to seek a subsistence in the Western World, where many a brave Scot has sunk broken-hearted and forlorn to his long home . . . .' But the story has a happy ending. After 1960 the British Transport Commission put the Caledonian Canal into fine shape and mechanised the locks. Fishing and light naval craft pass through, outnumbered in the holiday season by cruising boats. Britain's most scenic waterway will always be a charge on the taxpayer but, walking the towpaths, idling through in a cabin cruiser or driving the Great Glen beside it, most people would consider it money well spent.

WRITTEN IN THE STARS

From Spean Bridge a link road cuts through to Kingussie on the A9, passing Loch Laggan. In the loch is Eilean nan Con (isle of the hounds) and traces of kennels there are thought to be the remains of King Fergus's hunting lodge. Little is known about this early king of Scotland, though the following legend is attributed to him. Out hunting, he lay down to rest and fell asleep. A boar attacked and his dog defended him until he awoke and despatched it. To cure the dog's injuries, Fergus sent his seven daughters looking for a special herb. Six returned too late; the seventh returned empty-handed, having forgotten what she was looking for. The king placed his faithful dog in the sky – the Dog star – and banished his idle daughters there too: of the seven stars of the Pleiades, you will see one that is not very bright.

The scenery grows more dramatic by the mile as you proceed north towards Inverness. Tiny Loch Oich, at summit level, is a jewel. Fort Augustus is one of three military stations (Fort William and Fort George are the others) named for Georgian royalty and designed to keep the wild Hielandmen at bay. Its Benedictine abbey gives the lochside village a monastic, not warlike, atmosphere.

TWO CLASSIC MONSTERS

Half-way along Loch Ness, look over to the south bank. Boleskine House was the early twentieth-century home of Aleister Crowley, the black magician and self-designated 'wickedest man alive'. Then we are at Urquhart Castle, the ruin of a stronghold built by Edward I, the 'Hammer of the Scots'. It is the prime spot for sighting the Loch Ness Monster, and a mile away in Drumnadrochit is the 'official' Loch Ness Monster Exhibition, a collation of the evidence for Nessie's existence.

Was there ever, since the Tower of Pisa started to lean, such a gift to tourism as Nessie? Annually she fills the hotels and guest-houses of Inverness-shire with thousands who, but for her, would hardly venture this far north. The foreign tourist knows that if he hasn't seen Loch Ness he cannot pretend to have seen Scotland. Although that long, mysterious loch, the deepest freshwater lake in Britain, has a fascination all of its own, it is Nessie who put it on the map.

She needed no capital outlay. She requires no maintenance. She is eminently reproducible in pottery and in resin and on tea-towels and postcards. She is a free exhibition and costs the tourist authority absolutely nothing. She appears just often enough to keep people intrigued, but not so often that we get sick of her.

Sea-serpents are part of the folklore of all maritime nations. Inland, the world over, it is a very ordinary sort of lake which doesn't boast a legendary denizen. We have already met a couple at Strathmartine and Yetholm; Orkney has its Stoor Worm and Loch Morar is home to Nessie's cousin Morag. Nessie herself started out as a silly-season story in the *Daily Mail* in 1933, vouched for by a water-bailiff. The story snowballed with the discovery of a rich vein of superstition and reminiscence about Loch Ness, going back as far as the seventh century AD, when St Columba pacified a 'water-beast' and prevented it from eating a swimmer.

In April 1934 the first photograph appeared in the newspaper. Taken by a holidaymaker from London, it showed what could have been a flat head and a tapering neck, or the tail of a dolphin, or something quite different. A more recent picture, taken in 1977, is similar but suggests a small head and open mouth. There are a few dozen others and projective calculations based on the humps put Nessie's length at between sixty and ninety feet. Expensive expeditions with sonar and underwater cameras have turned up more, mostly showing unidentifiable blurs, probably fish shoals. Most pictures of Nessie have been denounced as fakes and there have been notable hoaxes, as when a practical joker under cover of darkness produced footprints with the aid of an elephant's-foot umbrella stand.

'Monster' in the dictionary is defined as 'an imaginary animal compounded of incongruous elements, e.g. centaur, sphinx, griffin'. Monster-hunter Steuart Campbell writes in *Loch Ness Monster: The Evidence* that Nessie, by the testimony of her viewers, 'is indeed an incongruous mix of reptile and mammal, of fish and amphibian . . . of seal, whale, eel etc.'.

Nevertheless, you will keep your eyes open and your camera at the ready as you follow the lochside to Inverness. Should she join you, by the way, as you are picnicking on the shore, have no fear. Folklore speaks of malevolent Nessies, prone to mangle sheep and carry off children. Over the years she has mellowed. These days everyone agrees that Nessie, the perfect tourist attraction, is a cuddly old pet.

URQUHART CASTLE: a favourite place on Loch Ness for monster-spotting.

13

INVERGARRY TO KYLE AND PORTREE

'Because of the remorseless clearing of the Glengarry estates,' writes Lorraine Maclean, '. . . there is little to be seen of interest along this road.' True, the first hard visitor attraction is thirty miles on in Glen Shiel, and that is no more than a car park and noticeboard. True, on a dull dreich day the landscape is a monotonous wilderness. But then the cloud cover lifts, a shaft of sunlight breaks through and the monochrome land comes alive with the

unreal colours of the badly touched-up postcard: fluorescent orange bracken, shimmering lochans of intense aquamarine – even the emerald peat bogs look inviting.

If not, it is in any case a small price to pay for where we are going: over the sea to Skye. Moreover, unlike the old military 'Road to the Isles' which Boswell and Johnson travelled, the modern route is well-surfaced, well-cambered, and has long straight

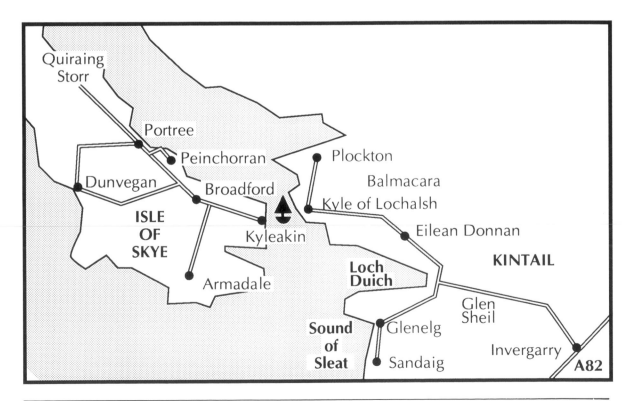

WEST HIGHLANDS: the wide-open spaces are one of Europe's few remaining wildlife refuges.

stretches for overtaking caravans. We can do the fifty-five miles to Kyle of Lochalsh in an hour.

Past Loch Cluanie, Sgurr na Ciste Dubh ('mountain of the black box') comes into view, the first of the Five Sisters of Kintail. The mountains belong to the National Trust for Scotland and range from 2800 to 3370 feet. In their shadow the battle of Glen Shiel was fought. It was a postscript to the 1715 Jacobite uprising: some opportunistic European armies saw a possibility of attacking England from the north and a Spanish force landed from frigates in Loch Duich. Joined by Rob Roy Macgregor, some of his clan, and an army led by the Earl of Seaforth, they got no farther than a few miles up the glen before government troops intercepted them.

BROCHS AND OTTERS

From Shiel Bridge we might make a detour to two tiny but famous places: Glenelg and Sandaig. The ascent over Mam Ratagan (sometimes spelled Rattachan) seems almost vertical. In a couple of miles you climb twelve hundred feet and the view over the Sound of Sleat to Skye is dramatic. From Glenelg in summer a ferry crosses to Kylerhea on Skye: in the days before sheep replaced cattle in the Highlands a swim across this quarter-mile of turbulent water was the prelude to a long trek to cattle markets in the south. Six thousand of the 'kyloes', as they were called, made the journey every year.

There are a few brochs in southern Scotland, but the far north and west have the greatest number. Dry-stane defensive dwellings, usually circular in plan, they were inhabited in early Christian times and before. The three near Glenelg are high on the list of antiquarians' favourites and among the best on the mainland.

A few miles along the hair-raising road to Arnisdale, a track leads off to Sandaig, former home of pioneering conservationist Gavin Maxwell who wrote *Ring of Bright Water*. Little remains of his burned-out house Camus Fearna, but Maxwell's ashes lie under a pink boulder and Edal the otter is buried under the nearby rowan tree. Britain's otter population has seriously declined in the last twenty years – pesticides are thought to be responsible – but there are still otters in this area, which doubtless

would please Maxwell more than if his house had been rebuilt as a heritage centre.

Eilean Donan is a great favourite with photographers. Sunset pictures of it are rarely absent from Scottish calendars and tourist board literature. The castle, built on the site of an earlier settlement of the Celtic monk Donnan (*sic*), was destroyed in Jacobite times. It was carefully restored in the 1920s and the small museum has various Jacobite relics.

LANDSCAPE OF BEWILDERING DIVERSITY

Not so long ago, in the elegant Georgian terrace in Edinburgh where the National Trust for Scotland have their head offices, Balmacara must have been a dirty word. It is, to date, the most expensive piece of litigation in the Trust's history. The Public Inquiry to resist on-shore oil-related development lasted forty-five days.

The 5000-acre Balmacara estate covers half the peninsula and includes the railway terminus and ferry port of Kyle of Lochalsh and the less-haphazardly planned town of Plockton. Laid out by Sir Hugh Innes to accommodate the victims of the Clearances, Plockton has a fine row of palm trees and rather too many holiday cottages. There are good views north towards Applecross where St Maelrubha came from Ireland to found a monastery. (A custom associated with the saint was the sacrifice of a bull on his day, until the seventeenth century when the practice was denounced as 'abominable and heathenish'.) Allow plenty of time if you detour to Applecross: there are many miles of single-track road.

From Balmacara, along a landscape and seascape of bewildering diversity we come to the Kyle ferry, a ten-minute shuttle to Kyleakin on Skye. Will the bridge ever be built? Since its proposal the letters page of the outspoken local paper, the *West Highland Free Press*, has been full of acrimonious dispute. Those who run the service industries on Skye have a vested interest in better communications. Those who don't, think the island is already too cluttered with tourists.

Cost is a factor. The ferry, like all those in the Western Isles, is government subsidised. Will a privatised bridge be too expensive to cross? The

GLENELG BROCH: that so many of these prehistoric dwellings survive is a testimony to the competence of their builders.

NTS's legal battles may not be over: the most obvious route for a bridge crosses their land and they have made it clear that the design must meet their approval. And where, 200 years ago, was the idle layabout Thomas Telford? You would have thought he could have taken a week or two off from building the Caledonian Canal to knock up a Skye bridge.

THE GREAT CURSE

Spring and autumn are the seasons to visit Skye. In summer the isle, irregularly shaped but about forty miles long by twenty across, is mobbed by visitors of every nationality. It is overrun too by the Great Curse of the Western Isles: the midge. A fortune, or at least a golden handshake from the tourist board, awaits the inventor of an effective deterrent, for this insect has ruined more holidays than the notoriously unsettled weather. The proprietory sprays on the market are no more use than a good cigar. As with its distant cousin the mosquito it is the female midge who bites. There are about 150 species, some, according to Para Handy, 'so big you could shake hands with them', and in an epidemic your best hope is to stay out of the forests and close to the beach, where there is usually a breeze. The midge cannot fly if the wind speed is more than 3 mph.

'There are certain scenes which would awe an atheist into belief,' wrote Thomas Gray after a visit to the Highlands in 1765. One such vista must have been the Cuillins. The jagged mountain range, dominated by Sgurr nan Gillean (3167 ft; the 'Peak of the Young Men'), usually wears an aureole of mist, the effect of the warm Gulf Stream brushing a cold land mass. There is nothing romantic about the corpses winched off it by helicopter every year. Climbing in the Highlands is not for the amateur. The weather will change from one extreme to another in minutes. Even a gentle hill walk should be approached with caution:

- Take heed of local advice and weather
  forecasts;
- Even on a sunny day dress as for the
  Antarctic;
- Leave behind your car windscreen a note of
  your route, with map references and your
  estimated time of return.

This is preaching to the sensible, but the sensible may be in a minority.

OLD MAN OF STORR

To the north of Portree there are physical features equally awesome. Off the A855 the Quiraing is a curious rock formation of pinnacles and hexagonal columns with a 120-foot obelisk known as the Needle. Before you reach it, Storr is a mass of craggy rock rising to 2360 feet, worth climbing on a clear day for an unforgettable view of the Outer Hebrides. The black column nearer the road is the Old Man of Storr.

Skye and the Hebrides are the last remaining outposts of the Gaelic tongue, though it is heard occasionally on Mull and in parts of the north-west mainland. Cynics say this language is as appropriate as Latin in today's world – but language is part of a map of a culture, a culture almost wiped out in the Clearances. Concerted effort by concerned individuals – preference given to bilingual teachers, for example – has prevented Gaelic from disappearing entirely.

THE CROFTERS OF GAELDOM

We look at some of the horrors of the Clearances in Chapter 18. During the nineteenth century almost all of Skye belonged to two families: the Macleods of Dunvegan and the Macdonalds of Sleat. Their atrocities are well-documented; ironically, the money to open the Clan Donald centre at Armadale, an award-winning visitor attraction, came from America, from descendants of evicted crofters. The presentation is well researched and carefully resists the usual temptation to glamourise history.

The same cannot be said of the restored 'black house' between Broadford and Portree. The tarted-up cottage evokes a cosiness entirely at odds with the miserable stinking hovels which nineteenth-century crofters called home. Take the turning to Peinchorran to see the stone which commemorates the battle 'fought by the people of the Braes on behalf of the crofters of Gaeldom'; an event which finally forced the government 600 miles away in Westminster to take action, fifty years too late.

THE FAIRY FLAG

The Macleods still live at Dunvegan Castle, open to visitors in the summer months. The gardens are outstanding and legend hunters will want to see the collection of Jacobite relics and the famous *Brattach Sith*, the Fairy Flag. It is supposed to have been brought back from the Crusades and given to a clan chief by his fairy wife. In a fable of the 'three wishes' variety, the Flag has the power to save the clan three times. It has already been waved twice in battle with success.

From the pier at Dunvegan there are boat trips to a nearby inlet, home to a seal colony. Depending on the season, you are likely to see hawks and herons as well as a hundred or more seals.

The wonders of Skye are spread out round the rugged coastline; Portree, the 'capital', is central to them. In 1819 Thomas Telford built the harbour and the row of cottages overlooking it. The oldest building is Meall House, formerly the jail and now the tourist information centre. Street names are in Gaelic and English and there are several hotels, including the Royal which is built on the site of the inn where Bonnie Prince Charlie and Flora Macdonald said their farewells.

Since the 1960s the island's economy has depended increasingly on tourism and every other croft seems to have a Bed-and-Breakfast sign outside it. As on Mull, there are too many holiday cottages, empty for fifty weeks in the year while young people born and bred on the island have been priced out of the market. There are many incomers too, referred to by locals as 'white settlers'.

In *Skye: The Island* James Hunter notes that most incomers are middle-class and English, inclined to meddle in local matters without properly understanding them. He tells of one who at a public meeting criticised the local farmers for killing the foxes which hunt their lambs. If the incomer in question did not like the way things were done on Skye, said the crofter, then he was quite at liberty to leave. 'And I'll be very pleased', he added with typical West-Highland courtesy, 'to show you the way to the ferry.'

BRAEMAR TO ABERDEEN, A93

Queen Victoria first visited Scotland as a young woman in 1842. Five years later her doctors persuaded her that the dry climate of upper Deeside would do her good and she bought a 'pretty little castle in the Old Scottish style'. Balmoral as a modest fortified hall such as the district abounded in did not suit Prince Albert at all. He had some of the grandiose ideas of his distant relation and

contemporary, the obsessive builder King Ludwig of Bavaria.

So he demolished it. Instead, he had built a new, double-rectangular block with connecting wings, fussy towers and a cupola: touches of aristocratic modernism as bogus as those by which Scott turned Clartyhole into mock-medieval-monastic Abbotsford on the Tweed. Balmoral's

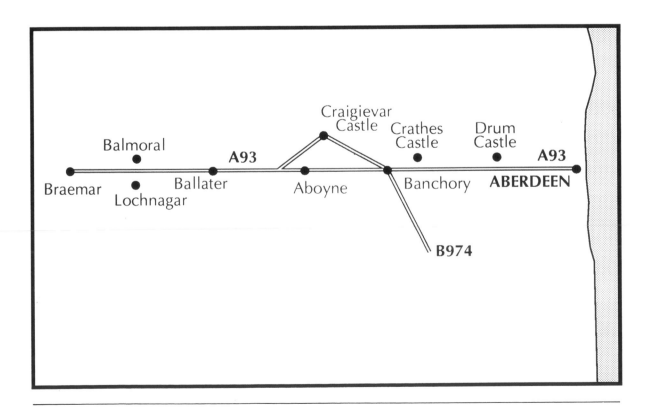

BALLATER: Highland cattle grazing by the 'town of the wooded stream', where half the shops have *By Royal Appointment* plaques.

ROYAL LOCHNAGAR DISTILLERY: an aerial view with Balmoral Castle in the background.

architectural excesses, however, are redeemed somewhat by the beautiful dove-grey granite, while the grandeur of their surroundings under dark Lochnagar cuts them down to size.

Our classic route to Aberdeen is a royal route. Royalty, British but often foreign too, has travelled the seven miles from Balmoral to the Braemar Gathering almost every year since 1848, the date Queen Victoria started going there. For her and her consort it was part of the romanticism of the Highlands which they vigorously promoted. Fascinated by kilts and plaids, by stag's antlers and bagpipes, they spread the so-called Highland fashion. (Many Highland folk had never seen tartan until they visited Royal Deeside.) Loyal inhabitants of the area stuffed the graceful greystone country houses and cottages for miles around with garish furnishings and impedimenta.

The historian Cuthbert Graham does not share this view. Commenting on a recently-published edition of the Queen's diaries, he writes: 'There is little excuse left for the wilful denigrators of Victoria who would attribute to her . . . a false cult of Highland romanticism.' He points out that Victoria was the first British sovereign for 250 years to acclimatise herself to Scotland. Here is an extract from the Queen's diaries: 'We were always in the habit of conversing with the Highlanders, with whom one comes so much in contact in the Highlands.' (Graham's pro-royalist leaning becomes more transparent when he writes of a current occupant of Balmoral as 'continuing the tradition of high skill on the moors'. No doubt he is correct in assuming that the red deer and grouse prefer a quick death to a slow one.)

Lochnagar above the distillery, retracing Byron's steps:

> *Though cataracts foam, 'stead of smooth*
> *flowing fountains,*
> *I sigh for the valley of dark Lochnagar.*

Useful cataracts these; made into whisky. Queen Victoria inspected John Begg's distillery in 1848 and granted him a royal warrant. (Prince Albert made Begg take several feet off the chimney; he claimed it spoiled his view as he sat being shaved every morning.) Tours of the Royal Lochnagar distillery and the visitor centre are free; a bottle of their best, Royal Lochnagar Special Reserve, costs just over £100.

Half the shopfronts in Ballater ('town of the wooded stream') sport *By Royal Appointment* plaques. Opposite the station, the end of the line from Aberdeen and where Victoria would disembark after twenty-four hours in the royal train, the tourist information office has a small museum of railway memorabilia. Not mentioned in railway histories, but firmly embedded in local folklore is the tartan train which transported the Queen's Messengers. The locomotive blossomed out in a coat of Stuart tartan, red, blue and white. It frightened the cattle in neighbouring fields, so it was changed to the milder Duff tartan, green and brown. Disused for thirty years since the Beeching cuts, the line awaits an entrepreneur looking to re-create a scenic royal steam railway.

Near Ballater is Craigendarroch, once the Highland retreat of the Keiller (marmalade) family of Dundee. Now an upmarket country club, it has everything, including a dry ski slope. It also has those most controversial of 1980s holiday developments elsewhere, timeshare lodges.

BY ROYAL APPOINTMENT

Take care on this section of the Deeside road. Every holiday motorist is looking for a glimpse of Balmoral and looking in vain. It is carefully screened from the main road by trees. For the best view, take the B976 ascending north from Crathie to the spot where the telephoto-toting *Sun* reporters foregather. The energetic will take the same road, but south, to climb

A SYMPHONY IN STONE

Ballater and the next town Aboyne hold Highland Gatherings like Braemar. Between the two we make an essential detour a few miles north into 'castle country'. Built between 1600 and 1626, Craigievar is a fairytale pink granite tower, a symphony in stone said to have inspired Walt Disney's drawings for the castle in *Sleeping Beauty*. Now in the care of the National Trust for Scotland, it was the home of the

CRATHES CASTLE: set in famous gardens .

Forbes family whose motto above the door reads: 'Do not vaiken sleiping dogs'.

Craigievar marks the transition from grim fortress to stately home. It has elements of both: lavish furnishings including famous plasterwork ceilings, while up in the turret there are gun ports for aiming muskets at enemies, attackers, Jacobean double-glazing salesmen and the like. It also has that essential pre-requisite of fairytale castles, the secret passage. Craigievar is thought to have been the work of George Bel, a master mason who lived and died in obscurity and who built several of the fine tower houses of Aberdeenshire. William Forbes ('Danzig Willie') was the first occupant; he made his pile as an Aberdeen merchant trading with the Baltic ports. Critics of granite, who say that only banks and tombs and nothing of elegance can be built with it, should visit Craigievar.

Next stop on the royal route is Banchory. This gifte-shoppe town has an air of net-curtain conservatism, but there are recent signs that it is dragging itself into the twentieth century. It is litter-free, however, and there are some attractive wooded walks down by the river. Close by is Crathes, another fine castle.

The Burnetts of Leys have had the lands at Crathes since 1323 and the castle and gardens were transferred to the NTS in 1951. Inside you can see the famous painted ceilings, the ivory horn given to the Burnetts by Robert Bruce as a token of ownership, and a 'tripping stair' designed to catch intruders. The gardens, really a series of gardens, contain exotic trees and shrubs and impressive topiary work on the three hundred-year-old yew hedges. Nearby, the renovated stable block has craftsmen in residence.

Leaving Crathes the A93 sweeps the last twelve miles into Aberdeen past Drum, another medieval fortress, and past the Camphill school which pioneers treatment and care of the mentally handicapped according to the philosophies of Rudolph Steiner.

THE GRANITE CITY

Aberdeen is famous for granite, gardens and oil: it is the 'floral city' and the 'Texas of the North'. Its first charter was granted by William the Lion in 1179 and the first guide book to the city was written in 1661.

The *Aberdoniae Utriusque Descripto* – written in Latin – earned parson James Gordon a silver cup, a silk hat, and 'ane silk gown to his bedfellow'.

The city has won the Britain in Bloom contest so often it is no longer allowed to take part. Rose beds divide the mile-long main thoroughfare Union Street, the Winter Gardens have the largest collection of cacti in Britain, and BBC Scotland's 'Beechgrove Garden' is in the suburbs. 'One detests Aberdeen', wrote Lewis Grassic Gibbon, 'with the detestation of a thwarted lover. It is the one hauntingly and exasperatingly lovable city in Scotland.'

Nothing remains of the thirteenth-century castle, destroyed by Robert Bruce to prevent an English garrison occupying it. The oldest buildings are the two university colleges and the two provosts' houses. King's College dates from the fifteenth century and the other three are sixteenth-century buildings. Marischal College, gleaming white and like a wedding cake left out in the rain, is built of Kemnay Granite, a stone which was exported to build the Paris Opera House and London's Waterloo Bridge. Provost Ross's House, built in 1593, has a doorway added a century later in the east wall so that John Ross could count his trading ships in the harbour. Provost Skene's House, which until this century was known as Cumberland's House – the duke stayed for six weeks on his way to Culloden – has a cycle of religious paintings in tempera, hidden for three hundred years under plaster.

THE SCOTTISH SAMURAI

The older part of Aberdeen is around the river Don. A favourite walk leads upstream from the river mouth through Cottown of Balgownie, in olden times a salmon-fishing community. Crossing the river by the Brig o' Balgownie, a beautiful Gothic survival, Don Street leads up to Old Aberdeen where the Cruikshank botanic gardens flourish on the site of the Gymnasium School where Thomas Blake Glover was educated.

Another Scottish 'lad o' pairts', Glover was born in 1838 and at the age of eighteen set sail for the Far East. In an extraordinary career he founded the Mitsubishi empire and designed Nagasaki harbour and the first Japanese warships. He was the first foreigner to be awarded the Order of the Rising Sun and the Glover Mansion is one of Nagasaki's tourist attractions.

What of the Aberdonians' legendary reputation for parsimony? It is said to have started quite accidentally, in a music hall song which rhymed 'Aberdeen' with 'mean'. Other countries have such scapegoat towns: Gabrovo in Bulgaria, where the citizens are supposed to take long strides to save shoe leather, is an example. But when, on the centenary of Robert Burns, a public holiday was declared throughout Scotland, the population of Aberdeen took only a half-day.

Through the 1970s and 1980s the city has had its problems, coming to terms with the influx of workers in the oil industry, for Aberdeen is the administrative and service centre for the North Sea rigs. Property prices in the city centre soared. Traditional family-run businesses disappeared overnight, replaced by nightclubs and wine bars. But the oil boom has peaked and the city is beginning to regain its rosy granite composure.

15

ABERDEEN TO INVERNESS BY ELGIN

There is no plaque outside the house in Ellon. No cairn, no monument. No award-winning, multi-media, audio-visual, state-of-the-art heritage centre.

Who needs Scottish heroines like Flora Macdonald, the misguided child who fell under Bonnie Prince Charlie's spell? Who needs Mary, Queen of Scots, described by Lewis Grassic Gibbon as having the 'face, mind, manners and morals of a well-intentioned but hysterical poodle'? Rock

superstar Annie Lennox, Ellon-born co-founder of the Eurythmics, most innovative musicians of the 1980s and major export earners, may one day be in the history books with Flora and Mary.

Perhaps one day there will be a Lennox Trail (her uncle was sometime Provost of Aberdeen). They are big on trails in these parts. Flushed with the success of the Whisky Trail, the marketing initiatives of the Castle Trail, the Quality Trail, the Victorian

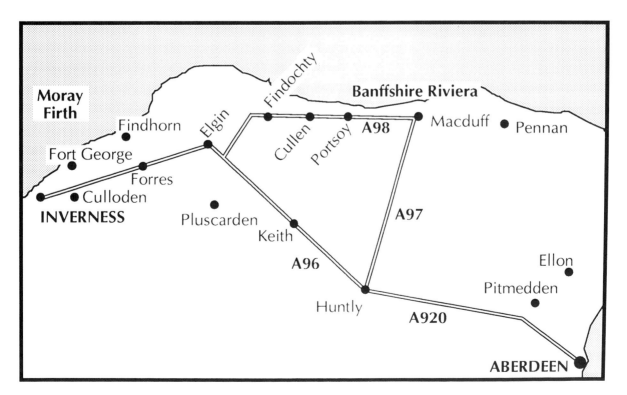

THE VICTORIAN HERITAGE TRAIL: 'Queen Victoria' in Fettercairn for the launch of a trail through Royal Deeside.

HUNTLY CASTLE: has heraldic enrichments and a facade modelled on a Loire château.

Trail and the Coastal Trail followed. Our classic trail crosses several of them.

Our first stop a few miles from Ellon is Pitmedden. We enter this jewel in the NTS's crown through a doorway inscribed 'FUNDAT 2 May 1675'. Sir Alexander Seton's split-level gardens are divided in the French style into four parterres, one of which is based on the Seton coat-of-arms. The twenty-seven sundials are said to be accurate to within ten minutes and the nearby museum of farming life has a growing population of rare breeds.

'SCOTCH' TOMATOES

North-west in relation to Elgin we skirt the edge of Speyside and the Whisky Trail, described in the next chapter. We can have a foretaste by following the A920 for a few miles to Oldmeldrum, where Glengarioch (pronounced 'Glengeary') distillery is open to visitors. Uniquely, the waste heat from the condensers is channelled into an acre and a half of greenhouses where pot plants and tomatoes – 150 tons a year – are grown. Staying with the A920, the route passes one of several stone circles in the district, at Loanhead of Daviot. Eleven standing stones enclose a burial cairn and date from before 2000 BC.

We pick up the main A96 for Huntly. The quiet county town on the River Deveron offers golf, fishing and pony-trekking. The splendid ruins of Huntly Castle span five centuries of Scottish history, from Norman motte-and-bailey to L-plan tower house. This former stronghold of the Gordon family has carved fireplaces, a heraldic doorway, and a French touch: the oriel-windowed front is copied from the château at Blois on the Loire, where the first Marquess of Huntly was governor while in exile.

BANFF: THE BATH
OF THE NORTH

Turning north on the A97 we make for the coast, where the twin villages of Banff and Macduff face each other across Banff Bay. ' . . . Only at Culcross in Fife and Banff in the north can tourist and antiquarian see a real olden Scottish town . . . endless quaint but solidly-built old houses,' wrote Sir Thomas Innes. Duff House, modelled on the Villa Borghese in Rome, is said to be a masterpiece of

William Adam. More likely it was a thorn in his flesh. Commissioned by the 1st Earl of Fife in 1735, it cost £70,000 (a huge amount) just to build the central block. Cracks appeared in the masonry and the earl refused to set foot in it, seeking compensation in law. Contractual problems were never resolved and Duff House remains incomplete.

THE BANFFSHIRE RIVIERA

Inverness lies west but we might detour east along the Banffshire riviera, past the 400-foot promontory of Troop Head to Pennan on the Aberdeenshire border. Pennan was a smugglers' haunt in the eighteenth and nineteenth centuries and lies on a fantastic coastline: instead of sloping down to the sea the land rises up to it, in waves of grassy hills.

West of Banff, there are more striking rock formations at Cullen, the gem of this riviera. By the grim ruin of Findlater Castle, Cullen has a beach of 'singing sands'. (Friction between uniformly spherical grains results in a curious noise when struck with a flat palm.) Portsoy, with its carefully-restored blocks of picturesque cottages, is a tiny port developed three centuries ago for the export of serpentine. This 'Portsoy marble' is to be found in the Palace of Versailles.

NORTHERN LIGHTS

Portknockie, Findochty, Buckie . . . those used to the buzz of city life may find these coasts desolate. In summer, along these miles of deserted sand dune the days are long. Golf courses are open to 11.00 pm. This coast is a prime spot from which to see the Aurora Borealis, the Northern Lights. The result of ionisation of gases in the atmosphere – nature's version of neon lighting – this stunning occasional effect spreads south from the Pole. Seek local advice: the residents can predict its appearance by the look of the evening sky.

We turn inland before the mouth of the River Spey, where the Tugnet Ice House has an exhibition on the river and its famous salmon. In Fochabers is Milne's High School, built in the Tudor-Gothic style. A footman of the Duke of Gordon's, Milne was dismissed for refusing to cut off his pigtail. He emigrated to America where he made a fortune as a

DUFF HOUSE, Banff: adjoining wings were never built because of a dispute between architect Adam and his client.

FORT GEORGE: Europe's largest Hanoverian fort, built after Culloden to keep the wild Hielandmen at bay.

builder in New Orleans, and in 1848 left a bequest of £100,000 to found the school. Just west of Fochabers, the family firm of Baxters has been canning fruit, bottling jam, smoking salmon and blending soups for more than a century. Tartan-clad guides give factory tours of the whitewashed building.

CHRISTIAN AND PAGAN

We are in Morayshire. Elgin's cathedral stands in roofless decay beside the River Lossie. New in 1270, it was accidentally burned out, then deliberately torched a hundred years later. Then the steeple fell down and the Earl of Moray stripped the lead off the roof to pay off his debts. Some fine thirteenth- and fifteenth-century architecture survives.

In 1390 the arsonist Wolf of Badenoch also turned his attention to Pluscarden, six miles south-west of Elgin on a minor road. The Valliscaullian Priory (see Beauly, Chapter 19) lay in ruins from 1560 until 1948 when Benedictine monks from Prinknash in Gloucestershire restored it. So far they have resisted the overtly tacky tourism of their English brothers and visitors can participate in services and see the Burghie Necklace, a jet Bronze-Age relic.

By contrast, the settlement at Findhorn is a pagan one. In the 1950s a young couple in search of spiritual enlightenment were 'guided' to this windswept, nettle-strewn patch of coastline, becoming neighbours of the fighter base at RAF Kinloss. Followers were attracted to their utopian dream and the Findhorn Community hit the headlines with stories, apparently genuine, of giant vegetables. By the early 1970s the site was filled with ramshackle caravans occupied with Californian hippies in search of 'meaningful experiences'. Today its supporters claim Findhorn is a social experiment of global proportions attended by lecturers of international repute. Go and see for yourself. Go and have a chat with the 'earth spirits' of their plants.

CASTLES OLD AND NEW

After Nairn the A96 turns inland. On your left, a castle. On your right, a fort. Still inhabited, Cawdor Castle was romantically linked by Shakespeare with Macbeth – but for historical accuracy the castle dates from around 1372, some three centuries after the

Thane of Cawdor was fighting for the Scottish throne.

The fourteenth-century descendant, according to legend, dreamed he would build a castle on the spot where the donkey carrying his box of gold stopped. The hawthorn tree where the donkey rested is still growing inside the guardroom. Apart from the central tower, most of the building is in the baronial style of the sixteenth century, complete with dungeon, well, spiral staircases and period furnishings; visitor tours are exceptionally well organised.

A very different fortification is Fort George, built on a spit which juts out into the Moray Firth. Military historians claim this as the finest eighteenth-century fort in Europe: it is certainly one of the largest. You can walk round the ramparts, a distance of over a mile. Begun the year after Culloden, this military base was completed in 1769 and is still occupied as an army barracks. A lavish visitor centre has a display of military uniforms throughout the fort's history.

Fort George marked the beginning of the 'civilising' of the Highlands. Leading up to the development of railways, the following hundred years brought a riot of transport improvements from Thomas Telford's canals and bridges to John Rennie's harbours to General Wade's roads.

> If you'd seen these roads before they were made
> You'd lift up your hands and bless General Wade.

The famous couplet is ascribed to Wade's deputy, Major William Caulfeild, who lived at Cradlehall Farm between Fort George and Inverness. He is reputed to have given lavish parties and the farm's name is said to derive from the cradle in which his servants removed inebriated guests to their rooms.

THE 'FORTY-FIVE

Much has been written about Culloden, the last battle on British soil. It was the bloody culmination of the third attempt to restore a Stuart to the throne of Great Britain and Ireland. It was also the beginning of the erosion and ultimate destruction of a social and economic order for which Whitehall could not or would not supply an adequate substitute.

The historian Gordon Donaldson notes that 'agreeable fiction always prevails over the historical truth'. Culloden was not a battle between the Scots and the English, or even between the clans and the Hanoverian army. More Scots fought under the Duke of Cumberland than for the Jacobite cause.

Having landed from a French frigate, Charles Edward Louis Philip Sylvester Casimir Maria Stuart, the grandson of deposed King James VII, raised his standard at Glenfinnan on 19 August 1745 in the presence of no more than fifteen hundred clansmen. A month later at the Mercat Cross in Edinburgh he proclaimed his father king. The Jacobites trounced unwary government forces at Prestonpans. They marched on London but by the time they reached Derby they had run out of steam. French reinforcements failed to materialise. Recruitment in southern Scotland was disappointing: the Prince's army numbered only 9000. Intelligence came of a large English task-force on its way back from the Continent. The Jacobites retreated.

On 16 April 1746, on the personal orders of Bonnie Prince Charlie and against the advice of his more senior commanders, the half-starved and travel-weary Jacobite army formed up to face the experienced, disciplined government forces led by the Duke of Cumberland who, like the Prince, was just twenty-five years old. It was over in an hour. One thousand Jacobites lay dying. Prince Charles Edward escaped: 'there you go for a damned cowardly Italian,' said Lord Elcho.

It is often regarded as a testimony to Highland loyalty that the Young Chevalier roamed the Highlands for five months uncaptured and with a price of £30,000 on his head – an enormous sum by contemporary standards. But the treasure chest was stolen. Escaping to Skye disguised as Flora Macdonald's maid, he ended his life in Italy, drowning his sorrows in French brandy.

Had he been captured, he might have entered a plea of entrapment at his trial. Undoubtedly he was set up by the French, who had no greater ambition than to create a diversion against the English. He was an inexperienced and incompetent military tactician. He was in the wrong place at the wrong time: the 1707 Act of Union, on its introduction as popular as today's Community Charge or 'Poll Tax', was by 1745 just beginning to show some tangible benefits.

In the middle of Culloden battlefield stands Old Leanach, a farmhouse which remarkably survived the fracas but has barely survived the attentions of the National Trust for Scotland who have a visitor centre here. For many, the whole site lacks atmosphere and fails to live up to expectations. So we will escape the crowds and the coach parties and go a little way south across the River Nairn to visit the Clava Cairns.

SOLSTICES AND SPACESHIPS

Wandering around these ancient structures set in a leafy glade, it is hard to miss the eerie atmosphere of timelessness. Cairns, brochs and standing stones present us with a major enigma of history. That so many have survived for four thousand years is a testimony to the competence of their builders, about whom we know virtually nothing. The chambered cairns are connected with burial rituals and the small or non-existent windows of the brochs suggest a defensive structure, but against whom or what?

The standing stones are even more puzzling. Explanations have been put forward which vary from the sublime to the ridiculous – for example that the stones were landing markers for extra-terrestial craft. The most popular theory, based on the accuracy of the stones' alignment, is that they were a calendar used by a now-extinct race to monitor the seasons in a fusion of agriculture, astronomy and religion. But as to the purpose of the 'pavement' at Clava, the curious grooves cut in stones, the depressions archaeologists call cup-markings, or even who these people were and how they lived . . . perhaps we shall never know.

16

THE WHISKY TRAIL

Our classic route is a unique one: the only Malt Whisky Trail in the world. You can cover the well-signposted circuit of about seventy miles in a day

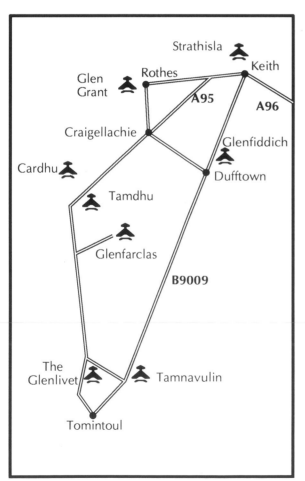

– though not if you stop at each of the eight distilleries – and even if you are not remotely interested in the subject of whisky our route takes in some unspoiled countryside and attractive little towns.

Whisky, from the Gaelic *uisge beatha* ('water of life'), in essence a distillate of beer, originated six or seven centuries ago as a sideline to farming. After Culloden and the Clearances which followed, the government realised they were missing out on a valuable source of revenue and slapped a heavy tax on it. The industry went underground – literally in many cases – until 1823 when the authorities abandoned their more extreme controls and began granting licences.

Towards the end of Victoria's reign the situation stabilised; then came Prohibition in America, the largest single export market. Tales of the distillers' efforts to beat the US coastguards are as legion as those of the crofters' attempts, a hundred years earlier, to beat the exciseman. During both world wars distilleries were closed down: the grain was needed for food and such spirit as was in bond was exported to fund the war debt: a scenario which provided the background for Sir Compton Mackenzie's comic novel, later a film, *Whisky Galore*.

Whisky's popularity waned in the 1970s as consumers switched to more fashionable 'white' liquors like vodka and gin. (Fashion is the sordid enemy of the consumer: today in London nightclubs people drink overpriced, inferior and immature bourbon, because it is the thing to do.) The recession

SPIRIT SAFE: quality and strength are carefully monitored under
Customs and Excise lock and key.

of the 1970s caused a number of distilleries to be
mothballed and the industry suffered from
outrageous trade protectionism in Japan where
Scotch carried a hefty import tax. Another problem
was poor imitations, like the cloudy and
understrength 'Loch Nest (*sic*), Finest Scotch
Whisky' as seen on French supermarket shelves.

Since the Whisky Trail opened in 1983 these
difficulties have been resolved. The industry is alive
and well, employs 200,000 people and earns more
than a billion pounds a year in exports. That so many

distilleries now have visitor centres is the result of the
only real change in the production process in a 150
years: individual distilleries no longer malt their own
barley on site – it is more economic to buy it in from
specialists – so the empty maltings are put to use as
whisky museums, whisky shops and visitor centres.

REGAL TIPPLE

Fifty miles west of Aberdeen, our starting point is
Strathisla, by the village of Keith. The distillery dates
from 1786 and although the single malt produced

THE STILL HOUSE: malt whisky is distilled twice before being stored in oak casks to mature.

here is not well known, it is an ingredient of a world-famous blend, Chivas Regal. Travelling south on the B9104 we pass Glenfiddich, a model distillery complete with duckpond and whitewashed buildings erected by William Grant, whose descendants are still in charge. The product, a twelve-year-old single malt in a distinctive three-sided bottle owes its success to relentless marketing. It is the biggest-selling single malt in the world, and indeed the *only* single malt sold in some expensive English hotels.

A SCOTCH-MAN AND AN IRISHMAN

Recent research indicates that 90 per cent of the population don't know the difference between malt and blended whiskies. To confuse the issue further, single grain whiskies have appeared on the market. Originally all whisky was single malt, made from malted barley in small quantities in a pot still. Then in 1831 along came an Irishman, Aeneas Coffey, with an invention which made continuous distilling possible. Mass production then dictated the use of other types of grain, and in a blend there can be as many as forty different kinds of malt and grain whisky. Blending produces a more consistent product – but the difference is between quantity and quality: single malts are to blends as vintage claret is to house red.

THE CLOCK THAT HANGED MACPHERSON

Rome was built on seven hills,
And Dufftown on its seven stills.

From Glenfiddich our route passes through Dufftown, a village of four streets meeting at a clock tower. This is the 'clock that hanged Macpherson', a reference to a local villain condemned to death. Public opinion demanded a reprieve, but the local sheriff advanced the hands of the clock to pre-empt the document's arrival and ensure that justice was done. The clock tower is now a local museum and tourist information office.

THE MILL ON THE HILL

Continuing south on the B9008 we pass the Tamnavulin distillery in the hamlet of Tomnavoulin,

spelling designed to confuse Sassenachs and typesetters alike. (Carelessness and illiteracy in the past have produced many shibboleths of spelling in Scotland: Atholl and Athole, Argyll and Argyle and so on.) Tamnavulin derives from the Gaelic for 'mill on the hill'; the distillery was once a carding mill. Passing Knockandhu we come to Tomintoul, at 1150 feet the highest village in the Highlands. We turn north-west here for a mile or so along the A939 and then north on the B9136 and follow the River Avon in the shadow of the Cromdale hills, whose peaty burns supply the essential ingredient of many world-famous brands.

THE BARLEY BREE

As befits an industry with a long history and tradition, myths and legends abound. One famous tale is set in the bad old days, when an exciseman and his confiscated barrel retired for the night to the upstairs bedroom of an inn. While he slept the distillers, who had followed him, drilled through the ceiling into the barrel and piped the contents into another cask.

More recently, when a hundred-year-old copper still reached the end of its useful life, the coppersmith was instructed to map and measure the dents it had acquired in service, and to replicate them so that the taste of the product was unchanged. Distillers have also developed their own vocabulary. On distillation of the *wort* (fermented mash), only the middle portion is kept, the *feints* and *foreshots* (first and last thirds) being discarded. The *angels' share* is the 25 per cent loss by evaporation from the cask, as the overstrength spirit sits for a legal minimum of three years – though a single malt will age for eight, ten, twelve, fifteen or more years.

Whisky off the still is colourless. Though caramel is often added to blended spirit, it is the cask which gives single malts their colour. Oak sherry casks are preferred, and from some distilleries the manager makes an annual trip to Spain to select his barrels personally.

Does whisky improve in the bottle? Probably not. It is not being conditioned like some beers or champagne which undergo a secondary fermentation. A single malt bottled in 1929 on sale at

MASH TUNS: Mr Richard Corns, the Head Brewer at Cardhu, supervises the early stages of whisky production.

CARDHU DISTILLERY: pagoda chimneys are a typical feature of distillery architecture.

Harrods recently would probably taste no better (or worse) than a single malt bottled last week, having spent ten years in a dusty, cobwebbed cask. Priced at £6000 it was of more interest to antique dealers than to whisky connoisseurs.

ETIQUETTE AND THE NIPPY SWEETIE

For detailed information on individual whiskies we refer to the excellent *Malt Whisky Almanac* by Wallace Milroy. What are we allowed, in civilised company, to put into whisky? Ice? No, it lowers the temperature which conceals the fullness of the aroma. Lemonade? Absolutely not. To quote the barman in a Highland hotel: 'It is deplorable to see the generations of tradition, skill, experience and subtle judgement that go into a successful blend wantonly sacrificed in one sugary moment.' In fact there is only one approved addition to whisky: water, preferably bottled spring water. Even soda water will, among the *cognescenti*, label you as a philistine. There is one small exception to this rule: when you return shivering and soaked to the skin after a day on the hills, we recommend you add a small, medicinal tot to a hot cup of coffee. The cure is an effective one.

NIPS AND DRAMS

Next on our route is The Glenlivet distillery: one of the first to show a public face, the visitor facilities here are comprehensively multilingual. Whisky has been made here since 1824 and Glenfarclas down the road was established in 1836. At Bridge of Avon we turn right for a few miles on the A95, then left on the B9012.

Close by the village of Cardow ('black rock') is Cardhu distillery. No red flag flies from its barn roof today. Helen Cumming, the wife of its founder, employed this technique to warn crofters that the excisemen were searching the hills. Across the road, the former railway station on the banks of the Spey is the visitor centre for Tamdhu distillery. Farther on we meet the A941, turn left and in three miles reach the village of Rothes, home to the Glen Grant distillery.

JOURNEY'S END

We have been to eight distilleries. There are more than 150 in Scotland, of which about thirty are open to the public. Like the wines of France, and although no two whiskies are the same, we can group them regionally. We have been travelling through Speyside, the area with the greatest concentration of distilleries and whose products we might classify as Highland malts. There are Lowland malts too – Blair Atholl, Glenkinchie, Glengoyne and others – which, in the language of the connoisseur, are more honeyed, more creamy than the sharper Highland malts. Then there are Island malts: peaty, smoky, kippery – Lagavulin, Talisker and Laphroaig, for example. To the uneducated palate they will taste of burning rubber. It is the great fascination of malt whisky that your tastes change with experience, that your palate can be educated. There is no better place to start than the Whisky Trail.

'Wait!' we hear you cry. 'Seventy miles and no whiff, aroma or bouquet of Thomas Telford?' Well, we would hate to disappoint you. Three miles back is one of Telford's major achievements, the Craigellachie Bridge. The main road crosses the Spey parallel to, and gives a good view of, the single span of Scotland's first iron bridge. At a cost of £8000 it was the most expensive bridge in the Highlands.

Of course these days you can pay almost that much for a bottle of whisky!

PERTH TO INVERNESS, A9

Northbound out of Perth our route passes close to the barracks of the Black Watch, the first British regiment to wear the kilt. Soldiers fighting eighteenth -century continental wars demanded, and got, an issue of long woolly stockings to wear under it, which seems to contradict claims for the garment's superior warmth and comfort. It's a dull road for ten miles, until we drop down to the densely-wooded valley of an old friend we have lost sight of, the River Tay. This is Birnam, where along the Terrace Walk a decrepit oak stands, the alleged survivor of a forest vandalised to provide camouflage for the army in *Macbeth*. Since Shakespeare's scenario was largely fictional, its authenticity is dubious.

A hundred years ago, after the railway came to Birnam, this part of Perthshire was the summer and autumn retreat of well-to-do families from London. The young Beatrix Potter spent her holidays here at Dalguise – a house, she noted in her diaries, built by a baker, who 'afterwards went to Australia and discovered a gold nugget, which was considered altogether more respectable'. Here Beatrix, surrounded by an environment rich in wildlife, wrote two picture letters in September 1893 which were later expanded into *The Tale of Peter Rabbit* and *The Tale of Mr Jeremy Fisher*.

Entering Dunkeld by Thomas Telford's bridge, observe the plaque. It commemorates Count Roehenstart of Bavaria, killed there in 1854 in a coach accident. The Jacobites claim him as the last direct descendant of Bonnie Prince Charlie, but farther north we shall meet two more.

Dunkeld's 'Little Houses', a National Trust for Scotland scheme, brighten the approach to the cathedral which, though much knocked about, sits as picturesquely on the river bank as do the border

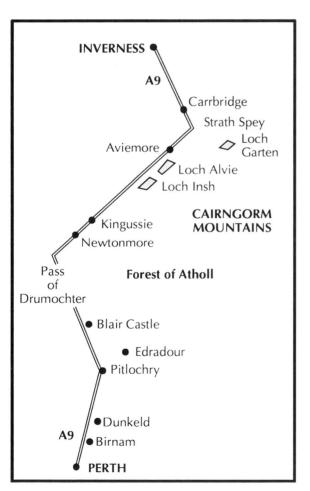

BAGPIPES: a skirl o' the pipes greets guests at the Station hotel in
Perth.

BLAIR CASTLE: the last castle on British soil to be besieged now hosts fiddle and piping competitions.

abbeys on the Tweed. We have searched the graveyard for Count Roehenstart without success. But you cannot miss the massive tomb, inside the cathedral, of the Wolf of Badenoch, the most ferocious robber baron of the Highlands. His very effigy makes you shudder.

OUT OF AFRICA

There is more to Dunkeld than meets the eye. If you have time, visit the ospreys on the Loch of the Lowes, two miles east. Here and farther north at Loch Garten, you can study them through binoculars provided on a viewing platform. May and early June are days of maximum activity as these annual visitors from Africa go through their post-natal routines.

The hen is perpetually dissatisfied with her dormitory. She plucks at the lining of the eyrie. She drags out a pleated pine branch, inspects it and puts it back. Her talons grasp a young log (how did she get it up there, forty feet above ground?). Standing back to admire the effect, she throws out a wing and now you have some idea of an osprey's size. It is as though on the coracle-shaped nest she has hoisted a black sail.

The car park on our route north, just outside Dunkeld off the bypass, is set in the forest of larches and cedars laid out by Planter John, Duke of Argyll, who introduced the former to Scotland 200 years ago. The trail leads to the Hermitage, a small Gothic retreat above the rapids of the Braan: a minor river but spectacular in its chasm after rain. Considering the Hermitage was once a major Highland sight, worth at least a page in the journals of early travellers, it seems a slightly anti-climactic little hideout.

PRIVATE ARMY

A scenic bypass on the Great North Road crosses a neck of land between Pitlochry and Loch Faskally. Pitlochry has more hotels than any other town of its size in Scotland, from Victorian mock-baronial to Highland cottage in style. In the main street, eager shoppers descend from coaches, hungry for the antique and souvenir shops, for woollens and terminal tartanitis. Other recreations include a visit to the windows of the Fish Ladder where salmon leap, and to Blair Atholl distillery: a model visitor centre

where the guides outnumber the distillery workers. Two miles out of Pitlochry through the village of Moulin is another establishment which makes malt whisky. The little whitewashed huddle of cottages at Edradour produces a mere 600 gallons a week, making it the smallest licensed distillery in the country.

Our visit to Pitlochry begins with a bang. Soldiers in pre-Culloden fancy dress are manoeuvring a piece of antique ordnance. The Master Gunner lights the fuse and tugs the lanyard. Nothing happens. They clear the touch-hole and he tries again. This time the charge blazes merrily in the barrel, which explodes. A few windows are broken and a photographer nurses his shattered camera. No matter. It takes more than a bursting cannon to disturb the morale of the Athole Highlanders, Britain's only private army. Its General, the Duke of Atholl, arrives, hedged in with the bonnets and claymores of a captain's escort, and proceeds to the main business of the afternoon, which is to open a restaurant in Pitlochry High Street.

THE SKIRL O' THE PIPES

Seven miles north, Blair Castle is the home of the Dukes of Atholl and headquarters of the Athole Highlanders and was the last British castle to be laid under siege. (In 1746 when its owner returned from campaigning with Bonnie Prince Charlie to find squatters had moved in he, laid siege to his own home.) The turreted white baronial castle plays host to numerous mock-military events and competitions, including the World Piping Championships.

'Is there a man with soul so dead, 'asks Jan Morris in *Scotland: Place of Visions*, 'that he does not thrill to the skirl of the pipes?' Yes, there is. A lone piper on a hillside half-a-mile away is tolerable; a massed pipe band is best enjoyed by the hard-of-hearing. Compared with their Irish or Northumbrian cousins, the Scottish bagpipes are strident and harsh in tone. History records that five Scots buried their bagpipes before going in to die in battle with Custer at the Little Big Horn . . . setting a fine example.

The fifteen miles from Pitlochry to Kingussie over the Drumochter Pass are among the bleakest in Scotland. Snow-gates at Drumochter indicate the severity of winters. Where the Atholl Sow and Boar of Badenoch (not mythical beasts but mountains) stand guard over the pass, the A9 picks up the infant River Spey and follows it through increasingly grand scenery under the heather-purple and snow-streaked Cairngorm massif.

IS ENGLAND STILL A MAN'S COUNTRY?

Newtonmore, just off the A9, is a straggling main street set in the characteristic valley landscape of river, birch wood, heath and pine; low-built cottages, fishing-tackle shops, tweed shops and a few Victorian granite villas standing back. Pony-trekking was invented here around 1954.

On the left as you enter from the south, at a dwelling known variously as the White House, the Red House, the Dower House and Bailabhadan, D. H. Lawrence spent the strike-bound summer of 1926. It was his only Scottish sojourn, his farthest north in a life of *vagabondaggio*. It rained continuously and he admitted to 'shrinking within the skin'. No wonder. He had just returned from Mexico, defying medical advice to stay in a dry hot climate, and he was a dying man. The only work he seems to have done was an article for the *Daily Express* entitled 'Is England still a man's country?' His hostess's niece relates that a copy of *Lady Chatterley's Lover* arrived with a thank-you letter. 'It was immediately ripped up by my grandfather and thrown on the fire.'

The Highland Folk Museum, a prototype of the genre, is at Kingussie and the Highland Wildlife Park, an offshoot of Edinburgh zoo, at Kincraig. Purists approve neither of zoos nor safari parks, but the former have this advantage over the latter: they don't normally attract litter, lager louts and sub-teenage hooligans. Scotland's safari parks have gone a long way downmarket. No wonder the animals look disgusted. Kincraig, so far, has escaped the worst of it.

THE SWAN CHILDREN OF LLYR

Past the imposing floodlit ruin of Ruthven Castle, once the home of the Wolf of Badenoch, there are two pretty lochans, each with an ecclesiastical legend.

Loch Insh is a RSPB bird sanctuary, occupied in winter by Bewick and Whooper swans. Perhaps they are descended from the Swan Children of Llyr, for the site of Insh church, known as the Swan Chapel, was here. Four children were turned into swans for 900 years by a wicked stepmother and in medieval legend turn up all over Europe, finally regaining their human forms only to die of old age in Connaught, Eire.

By Loch Alvie, the present church dates from 1876, though there are references to an earlier church (1107) which may have been the monastery of St Ailbhe. When it was refloored in 1880, 150 skeletons of soldiers buried with their weapons were found. They are now interred in the churchyard and a weathered stone commemorates a mystery:

> *Who they were, when they lived, how they died,*
> *Tradition notes not.*

It is well worth persevering with confusing signposts to seek out this peaceful haven just south of busy Aviemore.

QUEEN OF THE WHITE SPORT

Fifty years ago the Aviemore station-master asked a man disembarking from the night sleeper from Euston: 'What are those planks for?' The new arrival was carrying the first pair of skis seen on Speyside. Today Aviemore is the queen of the white sport and all-year leisure centre. The major hotel chains are represented in what was, within living memory, a couple of cottages, a post office and a railway halt.

Conferences and trade fairs keep the ball rolling. Like Inveraray, Aviemore polarises people. You either love it or you stay firmly on the bypass. The ski tows are east, on the Cairngorm slopes above little Loch Morlich, where you will find Britain's highest restaurant: fast food at 3600 feet. Lurcher's Gully is here too, a firm favourite in the acrimonious-controversy section of Scottish newspaper letters columns.

The part of the former Highland Railway between Aviemore and Boat of Garten, closed in 1965, was reopened in 1978 and volunteers and steam-rail enthusiasts at the Strathspey Railway are

LOCH ALVIE: a peaceful oasis off the A9. The church contains a curious historical enigma.

THE HIGHLANDS: rowans and birch trees thrive on poor soil and harsh winters.

working to extend the line to Grantown-on-Spey. The ospreys on the RSPB site at Loch Garten don't seem to mind: since they returned to Scotland in 1959 their numbers have been rising slowly. There are upwards of fifty breeding pairs; occasional egg thefts make headlines in the press. Thieves, if apprehended, face fines as huge as the sums the stolen eggs attract on the European market.

TREE MUSEUM

At Carrbridge, before we surmount the Slochd and run down to Inverness, the Landmark visitor centre was the first of its kind in Europe. It has grown from humble origins as a nature trail and timber exhibition area showing an audio-visual on Highland history. The maze and adventure playground with its aerial net walkways are a big hit with children and a recent development was the opening of a forestry heritage centre, including a sixty-five-foot viewing platform and a steam-engine-powered sawmill of a type common in Scotland half a century ago.

With Landmark as a prototype, perhaps the 1980s will be remembered as the decade of the heritage centre across Britain. There are big bucks to be made selling nostalgia. Do we need more audio-visuals, more interpretative displays? Is history enhanced by being packaged, labelled, sanitised and given the hard sell? Do we need to be told, by means of the latest in laser technology, what a tree is?

We leave Landmark, where coaches from Wigan and Wetherby jostle for position in the car park, and go on in search of the real essence of Scotland, the wide open spaces.

18

INVERNESS TO JOHN O'GROATS, A9

It lay in a drawer at the Town House for fifty years, but now they have framed it and put it on the wall: a plain sheet of paper with twelve signatures on it, the

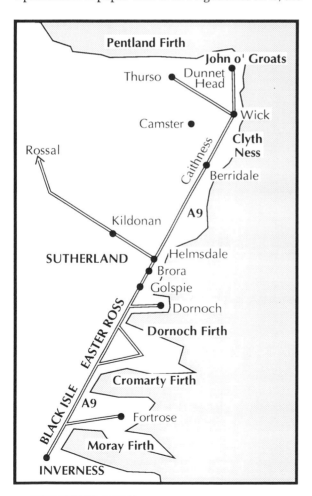

sederunt of the only British Cabinet meeting held outside London. Between a florid 'David Lloyd George' at the top and a self-effacing 'Winston S. Churchill' at the bottom, you make out the names of Birkenhead, Baldwin, Chamberlain, Geddes and others.

In September 1921 the Irish question came to a head. An emergency Cabinet was called. Lloyd George was at Flowerdale, fishing. Several ministers were shooting grouse in different parts of the Highlands. King George V was staying at Moy, ten miles down the road from Inverness. That was how the Highland metropolis came to be chosen for the meeting. And how fitting, said *The Times*, 'that this thorny Celtic question should come under review in an old Celtic capital, rich in Celtic memories, and that the deliberations should be presided over by the Prime Minister, himself a Celt of Celts'.

All the tourists for miles around flocked into Inverness. At least, in that somnolent, introverted little town, something was happening. The ministers came by motor car or off the early train. Some wore morning coats and top hats, others hacking jackets and deer-stalkers. Lord Birkenhead, summoned from the south of France, sported a yachting cap. A wave of cheering travelled through the street ahead of what was rumoured to be Lloyd George's Rolls Royce – and waves of laughter billowed out as the crowds parted to let through, not His Majesty's first minister, but an errand-boy trundling a barrowload of beer crates.

Late in the afternoon the Sinn Fein representative was called in. He left with a note for Mr de Valera, foreshadowing an even greater day for

CLYNLISH, SUTHERLAND: most of the north of Scotland was savagely depopulated in the Highland Clearances.

Inverness, nothing less than a peace conference a fortnight ahead. The ministers dispersed. Last to leave were Lloyd George and Winston Churchill, who drove off together to Lord Seafield's house at Brahan.

The Treaty of Inverness never got into the history books. The Irish insisted on the status of envoys of a sovereign power, to which Britain could not agree. The Cabinet meeting might just as well not have taken place.

SCOTLAND'S NOSTRADAMUS

Crossing the River Ness to pick up the A9 for Sutherland and Caithness reminds us of the Brahan Seer. Scotland's Nostradamus prophesied world catastrophe if ever a fifth bridge was built over this river. In August 1939 a temporary bridge was put up, making five. Hitler marched into Poland a couple of weeks later.

The Seer had the track record that most soothsayers have: he was as often wrong as right. He also came to a hot and sticky end, boiled in tar by the Countess of Seaforth whose husband's infidelity the Seer had 'seen'. An eight-mile detour from the A9 to Fortrose on the Black Isle will take you to the cairn that commemorates him.

Beyond the Cromerty Firth we take the short cut over the Struie in preference to the A9 through Tain. It is a breezy moorland road with a famous drovers' inn at Aultnamain and breathtaking views of the Dornoch Firth on the descent. 'Traveller STOP', insists the plaque beside Bonar Bridge, 'and read with gratitude the names of the Parliamentary Commissioners appointed in 1803 to direct the making of above Five Hundred miles of Roads through the Highlands . . . .' The bridge we cross today is the third; the first, destroyed by flood in 1892, was the work of Thomas Telford.

At Bonar Bridge we enter Sutherland which, with Caithness, is the wildest and most rugged part of mainland Britain. The Romans never made it this far. The Picts, and whatever civilisation preceded them, have left here, as in Orkney and Shetland, a staggering number of standing stones, chambered cairns and carvings. Centuries of Norse rule have bequeathed distinctly Scandinavian place-names. (Norway owned Orkney and Shetland well into the Middle Ages and still has an option on them.) But the character of Sutherland and Caithness today owes as much to the Clearances as to any other historical event. That inscription at Bonar Bridge (like the one on the Duke of Sutherland's monument to which we are coming) has ironic overtones. Those 'Five Hundred miles of Roads' facilitated the Clearances.

SUTHERLAND'S LAW

Now that the dust has settled, opinion on the Clearances is divided. It is argued that, sooner or later, the inhabitants of the far north of Britain would have had to be dragged out of their squalid existence and persuaded to abandon an out-moded and insupportable lifestyle. But sentimentalists and nationalists are still bitter about the Clearances, regarding them as an act of revenge by a foreign king and a faraway Establishment against those clans who had supported the Jacobite claimants to the British throne.

What is true about the Clearances is that innocent people suffered while rich and greedy men got richer; and that the law was flouted outrageously – today's civil rights lawyers would have had a field day. After the most brutal of evictions, when the scandals became generally known and something had to be seen to be done, the guilty were put on trial – and acquitted.

In 1813 the Duke of Sutherland's factor, Patrick Sellar, had begun the clearance of Strathnaver. 'Many deaths ensued from alarm, fatigue and cold,' wrote Donald Macleod, an eyewitness. In 1816 Sellar was tried at Inverness on charges including arson and oppression. A jury of landowners acquitted him. Then the law turned its attention to Macleod, the outspoken critic. His family was harassed and evicted and he himself was branded a debtor. Reunited with his family, he moved to Edinburgh and continued to put pressure on the authorities via the newspaper columns.

Forty years later the forcible depopulation of the glens was continuing. After a visit to Strath Carron, just west of Bonar Bridge, a Glasgow lawyer named Donald Ross reported that 'more than twenty females were carried off the field in blankets and litters; and the appearance they presented, with their heads cut and bruised, their limbs mangled and their clothes clotted with blood, were such as would horrify any savage.'

Thousands annually make their dewy-eyed pilgrimage to Bruce's statue at Bannockburn, a monument to brute force and a dagger between the right ribs. Very few seek out the Highland hamlet of Rossal, where Donald Macleod was born. In his day, thirteen families eked out a meagre existence, but it has been deserted ever since the Clearances. Another historian, James Miller, notes that it takes only twenty minutes to walk round Rossal . . . 'a walk every landowner in the Highlands should be made to take'.

COASTAL FORTS AND
STATELY HOMES

Before we leave Bonar Bridge on the A9 we might detour a few miles north on the A836 to view Carbisdale Castle in its lordly setting amid woodland above Invershin. This is our introduction to the great ducal family of which we cannot escape being reminded as we tour the far north. Towards the end of last century, the Sutherlands' domestic affairs looked to be as stormy and distressing as those of their outlying tenants, earlier on, had been. At one stage the Dowager Duchess served forty days in Holloway Jail for contempt of court. After years of inter-family feuds, the duke bought his lady off by building her a castle of her own – and she made sure it was a good one. They say that when he rolled past Carbisdale in his train he had the blinds drawn to avoid seeing it. But the Castle was destined for quite a plebeian fate: it is now a youth hostel, albeit the largest and most lavishly-furnished in the country.

Sutherland at first glance looks like a fruitful and prosperous county. The A9 along the firth from Bonar Bridge has something of a Riviera atmosphere. The ruined mill at Spinningdale is a reminder that not all the lairds tried to solve their economic problems by driving people away: George Dempster of Skibo, with the backing of David Dale of New Lanark, built the mill to provide employment for a hundred workers and at one period Mackintosh the inventor of waterproof cloth was associated with it. But its remoteness from the markets eventually forced its closure. At Skibo Castle, a few miles on,

hidden from the main road by forest, the billionaire steel baron Andrew Carnegie entertained top people, including King Edward VII. The Castle has recently passed into the hands of another tycoon, Peter de Savary.

'As you love me you shall love the monks that live at Dornoch in Caithness [actually in Sutherland],' wrote David I to the Earl of Orkney in the twelfth century. After the saintly David's death, Norse invaders landed nearby at Embo, the 1st Earl of Sutherland captained the defending army and in the thick of battle lost his sword. He seized the nearest weapon, the severed leg of a horse – which accounts for the horseshoe on Dornoch's coat-of-arms. Dornoch has the distinction of having got rid of the last Scottish witch. In 1722 Janet Horn, found guilty of turning her daugher into a pony, was tarred, feathered and burned.

Clean sandy beaches and a sizeable caravan park testify to Embo's popularity as a holiday resort. The remains of a chambered cairn stand in the grounds of the Grannie's Hieland Hame Hotel – a name perhaps for the younger generation of visitors to conjure with, but elderly Scots remember when *Grannie's Hieland Hame* was as mandatory a part of the drunk's repertoire of songs as is now another mawkish piece of drivel, *Flower of Scotland*.

The next coastal fortress is Skelbo Castle. Here, in the thirteenth century, envoys anxiously awaited the ship bringing Margaret the Maid of Norway, heiress to the Scottish throne. The third girl died on the voyage, possibly of sea-sickness, and the path of Scottish history made another sharp detour.

On the skyline of Ben Vraggie you will see (you can hardly miss it) the towering monument to the 1st Duke of Sutherland. The 'MOURNING AND GRATEFUL TENANTRY' who, according to the inscription, erected it did not presumably include those dispossessed wretches sailing westward in the emigrant ships.

For some distance after Golspie the A9 skirts the woods and parkland of Dunrobin Castle, the duke's principal residence. It was designed by Sir Charles Barry (who also designed the Houses of Parliament) in the style of one of the more ostentatious French châteaux. Sentence of democratisation has been passed on this castle, too: it

THE BRAHAN STONE, Fortrose: the Seer was Scotland's Nostradamus and foresaw the outbreak of World War II.

is scheduled for touristic development along the lines of the funfair stately homes of England, such as Woburn Abbey and Alton Towers. No need to build a miniature railway, the Duke already has one *in situ*.

From the time they were invented, trains fascinated the Dukes of Sutherland; unlike their northern neighbours the Dukes of Portland, who couldn't bear trains. This is why, throughout the transit of Sutherland, road and railway proceed affectionately intertwined along the scenic coastline and, as soon as they reach the Langwell estates in Caithness, the railway takes a wild swing inland, serving nothing and nowhere in a great arc of desolation before returning to the coast at Wick.

For some years the line's terminus was Helmsdale on the Sutherland-Caithness boundary. In 1871 the parties met at Dunrobin to discuss the extension to Wick and the engineers decided that the Portlands would be more of a hazard to progress than the unstable peat bogs of the Flow Country. So the seventy-five-mile detour was agreed and in 1874 the Duke of Sutherland drove his private train over the whole route in four and a half hours.

Railways were bad news for the peasants. They opened up the north to the pastimes of the rich: shooting, fishing and deer-stalking. The transformation of large areas, not exclusively in Sutherland, into recreation grounds for well-heeled shooting tenants and anglers led in 1882 to the Land League, a pressure group, obtaining a government commission of enquiry into land use in the Highlands. The five large volumes of recommendations which it produced are the basis of today's crofting legislation. Ironically, the Duke of Sutherland's son stood for Parliament in 1884 on the issue of land-use reform. (He seems to have been the typical rebel son: he also advocated nationalisation of land and the abolition of the House of Lords.)

Today, when pop stars and media personalities try to buy large chunks of Sutherland as a tax dodge, they get short shrift. But when you stop for a picnic beside a lonely moorland road you still run the risk of having a ghillie appear from nowhere and order you to move on because you are disturbing the grouse.

At Clynish, the only distillery in Sutherland, a superior whisky is produced. Another unique feature of the district is the coal mine at Brora. It became uneconomic in the 1970s but surveys have shown remaining seams of eight million tons. Coal has been won at Brora since the sixteenth century. We are asked to believe that the old miners used phosphorescent fish-heads for a lighting system.

Next century it may well be liquid gold which will shape the north of Scotland's economy. Twelve miles out to sea off Clyth Ness is the Beatrice oilfield. But there is real gold at hand on the very rim of Sutherland. A short detour from Helmsdale (in Victorian times an important herring port, with a harbour by John Rennie) takes us to the Baillie an Or at Kildonan, where £12,000 worth of gold was panned in the 1868 rush before the Duke of Sutherland, irritated by the conduct of the prospectors, withdrew the licences. A few years ago the local hotel started advertising gold-panning holidays, picks and sieves provided.

CAT PEOPLE

Beyond Helmsdale we cross the Ord of Caithness, a county which may derive its name from the Norse *Katanes*, land of the cat people. The road rides high over the Ord and the sea horizon looks far off. Berriedale, tucked into its narrow combe and for years, until the road bridge smoothed out the descent, assailed by lorries whose brakes were for ever failing, suggests a landscape Devonian in character. It is untypical. Scenically, Caithness is a dull region, mile upon mile of dispirited tussocky grassland. Far from resembling Devon, it reminds you of the midland bogs of Ireland.

They call it the Flow Country and that seems appropriate when you cross it, as you usually do, in a gale of wind. The whole landscape appears to be on the move. Rivers of hay, flowing out of disintegrating mounds of winter fodder, tear across the road. The stunted bushes that pass for trees in this part of the world become miniature haystacks themselves, bent under vagabond grasses, gorse and heather swept down by the storm. Only the whitewashed, turf-thatched farm cottages stand firm. You no longer see or hear the sea, it is invisible under clouds of foam and inaudible beneath the roaring of the wind.

Whenever you dip down to negotiate a coastal village you imagine that its foundations are shaking and when you climb out again you have to stop to scrape the salt spray from your windscreen.

At least the road has undergone some improvement: you can see the old one here and there, described by Bishop Robert Forbes in 1762. 'Its Steepness,' he said, 'and being all along the very Brink of a Precipice, are the only Difficulties.'

At Langwell we pass the home of another north-country 'improver', Sir John Sinclair, who argued in 1795 that a landowner was 'properly a Trustee for the public'. The Sinclair estates 200 years on have a viable industry in deer-farming and most recently in the bottling of spring water for aquaholics.

After Dunbeath, another village tucked into a cove where Neil Gunn the novelist (1891–1973) was born, we come to Lybster, once the third herring port of Great Britain, now an insignificant spot. North of the village an unclassified road leads to Camster, where there are two chambered cairns around 5000 years old, while farther on along the A9 at Mid Clyth on the Hill o' Many Stanes more than 200 boulders are arranged in twenty-two parallel rows.

END OF THE ROAD

Our old friend Telford designed Wick harbour, where white fishing is still important although the herring boom is over. Some idea of the size of the population in Telford's day is revealed in the diary of a contemporary minister, which reported that 500 gallons of whisky would be consumed after a successful day's fishing. But half a century later Wick appeared to R. L. Stevenson the 'meanest of man's towns'. The future novelist, then in his teens, was touring the east-coast ports as part of his apprenticeship to civil engineering, the profession of his father and grandfather.

In Telford's time the governor of the Fisheries Society was Sir William Pulteney, a name perpetuated in the Old Pulteney single malt whisky made at Wick. Underwater cameras are made here too, by one of the world's leading manufacturers. So is the venerable and much-prized Caithness Glass, of which the BBC's annual 'Mastermind' trophy is made.

Two hundred and fifty miles back, and twelve chapters ago, we started from Edinburgh on our longest classic route. Now we are on the last leg, seventeen miles to John o' Groats. At Auchengill we might pause at the small museum devoted to one of Scotland's more obscure heroes: John Nicholson, farmer, painter, sculptor and amateur historian. But the name most tossed about on Scotland's northern fringe these days is that of no local worthy but an incomer: Peter de Savary who, having already acquired Land's End, now owns John o' Groats. (Did he believe, as so many do, that that was the northernmost point of mainland Britain? It does not quite touch the latitude of Dunnet Head, ten miles west, a much better bet for a playground, with its fine headland, broad arc of firm pale sand and astonishingly warm water – either from the Gulf Stream or nearby Dounreay – than the ugly sprawling shanty encampments which disfigure John o' Groats.)

The name comes from Jan de Groot, a Dutch settler who ran a ferry to Orkney from the beach below the point where the A9 now ends. The Dukes of Sutherland might have taken tips in diplomacy from the legend of Jan de Groot: he is supposed to have built a house with eight doors and a table with eight sides, to give members of his family equal rights in the domestic situation.

Crossing the Pentland Firth in those far-off times must have been an exciting experience; it still can be. Through one of the roughest sea-straits in the world the tidal stream runs at ten knots or more and, in sailing-ship days, mariners would go a long way round Orkney to avoid it. Freaks of turbulence, like the Merry Men of Mey (a stone's-throw from the Queen Mother's Castle of Mey) and the Swelkie, a whirlpool (Norse *svelgr*), are sometimes visible from the shore. The old legend of 'Why the Sea is Salt' attaches to the Swelkie. Mysing, the Norse pirate, stole a magic quernstone and set it to grind a little salt for his meal. (Compare the story of Michael Scot in Chapter 3.) Mysing couldn't stop it. The mountain of salt sank his ship and the quernstone continues to grind on, creating the Swelkie and manufacturing salt.

CAMSTER CAIRNS, CAITHNESS: associated with burial rituals, but many archaeologists' questions remain unanswered.

19

INVERNESS TO ULLAPOOL

We cross the Ness at Friars' Bridge and the Caledonian Canal below Muirtown Locks. A lengthy eulogy by Poet Laureate Robert Southey commemorates the opening of Telford's canal in 1822; the words are inscribed on the wall outside Clachnaharry House, now the canal headquarters.

Structures of more ambitious enterprise
Than Minstrels in the age of old Romance
To their old Merlin's magic lore ascribed.

This is the A862 and we are going west. Before the Kessock Bridge was built, the road was the A9, taking us round Beauly Firth before turning north. Seen in the firth at low tide is the little artificial island of Carn Dubh, one of five crannogs (prehistoric lake dwellings). A little farther on, those interested in wine will want to make the short detour to Moniack Castle, a seventeenth-century tower house and stronghold of the Frasers. Wineries are uncommon in Scotland: the recent enterprise at Moniack makes

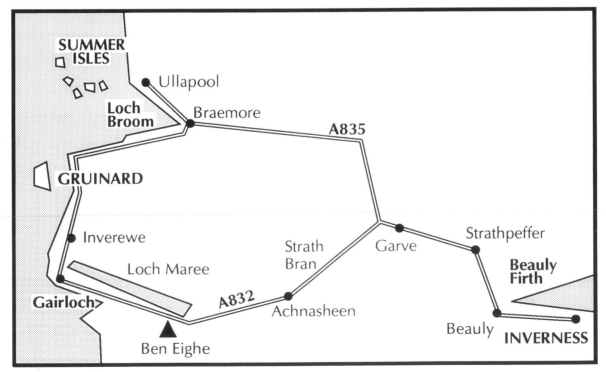

wine from birch sap by tapping the trees in spring. There are also fine trees at nearby Reelig Glen, planted around 1800 and given to the Forestry Commission this century by the Frasers of Reelig.

OF CABBAGES AND KINGS

We pass Highland Craftpoint, a crafts information service which has exhibitions in summer and runs training courses in winter, and then we are in Beauly. The Gaels called it Manachain, the place of monks. The monks called it Bellus Locus, which via Beau Lieu became Beauly.

The Valliscaulian order is an unusual one: there are only two other of its houses in Scotland, including Pluscarden founded by Alexander II. The word means 'valley of the cabbages' and derives from the mother house at Val des Choux in France. It merged with the Cistercians in 1757 but Beauly Priory dates from 1230, though much of it was later rebuilt. The monks also built a harbour which was in use until the early years of the present century. The neat little town of today was laid out to a rectilinear plan by Thomas Fraser, who became Lord Lovat in 1837.

YOUNG PRETENDERS

Right-wing romantics may want to detour to Lord Lovat's Roman Catholic church at Eskadale, where the two Sobieski Stuarts are buried. Were these young men really the last descendants of Bonnie Prince Charlie? Among latter-day Jacobites, champions have not been lacking – nor sceptics who consider them impostors. The debate continues.

John Sobieski Stuart, alias the Chevalier, aged about twenty-two, and his brother Charles Edward, aged about nineteen, first appeared in Scotland in 1818. Their father was a naval lieutenant living in London, a shadowy figure whom no one managed to see or correspond with. He was officially the son of Admiral Allen but rumour said he was actually a royal personage, smuggled aboard the Admiral's flagship as a baby during political disturbances in Naples; none other than the son of Bonnie Prince Charlie.

The brothers were Allan (*sic*) when they came to Scotland. They rapidly became Allan-Hay, Stuart-Allan-Hay, Hay-Allan-Stuart and finally Stuart. The Scottish establishment was uneasy about them: new

Pretenders appeared every few years. But old Catholic patriarchs like the Lovat Frasers and the Crichton-Stuarts met them and were conquered. These young men bore a striking resemblance to youthful portraits of Bonnie Prince Charlie. They certainly had the Stuart love of finery and ceremony. They spoke the Gaelic. They specialised in clan history and clan costume and in due course published costly books illustrating the chivalry of Highland lairds past and present, which further endeared them to their Scottish hosts.

During their visits to London they were seen at the British Museum, gorgeously attired, wearing swords and spurs, engaged on their researches at a table specially equipped for them with coroneted pens and ink bottles. In Scotland they lived as honoured guests at Inveraray Castle and Beauly House near Dingwall. The full Highland dress, festooned in sashes, ribbons and orders, was their everyday wear. Crowds gathered on Sundays to see them leave the lodge Lord Lovat had built for them, embark in boats with their personal pipers and proceed to church, where local gentry kissed hands, ladies curtsied and everyone retreated backwards from their presences.

They lived on hospitality and handouts until 1872, when John Sobieski died, and 1880, when Charles Stuart died. They were hopelessly insolvent. Menzies the Edinburgh bookseller was never paid for the copies of *Costumes of the Clans*, at seven and a half guineas a time, which he had despatched thirty years earlier at the brothers' request to the crowned heads of Europe. That book is now very rare, but the public library in Inverness has a companion volume, *Vestiarium Scoticum*.

SO DELIGHTFUL TO MY SOUL

At Muir of Ord we take the A832 for Strathpeffer. The Victorian spa resort was well established when R. L. Stevenson visited in 1880: 'No country – no place was ever for a moment so delightful to my soul.' Back in 1819 a doctor, Thomas Morrison, discovered the value of the natural sulphur and chalybeate springs and persuaded a local landowner to build a wooden pump room – later replaced in sandstone – over them. The railway came in 1862 and by the turn

THE PUMP ROOM, Strathpeffer: 'No place was ever so delightful to my soul,' wrote Robert Louis Stevenson.

ULLAPOOL: purpose-built fishery town still has a fleet, though most of the catch is sold at sea to Eastern-bloc factory ships.

of the century there was a daily service to and from London. But by the outbreak of the First World War spas were going out of fashion, and today the station with its cast iron and glass canopy houses a visitor centre and craft workshops.

Plans are afoot to develop a narrow-gauge railway to the summit of Ben Wyvis (3429 ft) though local residents – golden eagles, buzzards and red deer – may well view this intrusion with disfavour. Legend has it that snow lies all year round in a gully atop the mountain, and that it was a condition of tenancy of a neighbouring estate that a snowball could be produced at any time on demand.

Strathpeffer and Strathconan are rich in golf courses and hotels. Other attractions include the Falls of Rogie, where from a suspension bridge you can see salmon leap; the Eagle Stone, a Pictish slab with carvings of a horseshoe and an eagle; and the tiny Museum of Toys and Dolls, a collection spanning 150 years which occupies a room in its curator's house.

RAILROAD TO THE ISLES

From Strathpeffer we retrace our steps for a couple of miles and pick up the A835 to Garve. Garve station is on the famous route from Dingwall to Kyle of Lochalsh, arguably the most scenic railway in Britain and nearly axed in the Beeching cuts of the 1960s. Trains haul observation carriages and are occasionally steam-driven on this classic rail route. Out of Garve we have a choice. Both A835 and A832 go to the same place, Braemore, but whereas the former speeds us along Loch Glascarmoch for twenty miles, the latter describes a huge arc of ninety. Our appetites for majestic mountains and savage scenery persuade us on to the longer route.

TO THE ICE MOUNTAIN

Is Strath Bran haunted by a canine ghost? Bran, the mastiff of Celtic hero Finn McCool, who crops up in Irish legend as well as Scotch myth, was described as having yellow paws, a green back, red ears, black flanks and a white belly. This multicoloured monster must have been recognisable from some distance. We part company with the railway at Achnasheen and head for Ben Eighe, the mountain of ice. The nine peaks of Torridonian sandstone are 750 million years

old and were the first National Nature Reserve so designated in Britain. But they are mere adolescents compared with the Lewisian gneiss (pronounced 'nice') of north-west Sutherland: aged about 3000 million years, it is the oldest part of Britain.

Loch Maree is a geological fault, where water has accumulated in a basin scooped out by ice. The little Isle Maree has the ruins of a chapel, said to be the hermitage of St Maelrubha, and his well where by tradition visitors have left coins pinned to trees. Queen Victoria followed this custom during her visit in 1877, presumably leaving her portrait.

There are scattered attempts at re-afforestation. Once, the whole north of Scotland was covered by the great Caledonian forest. During the Industrial Revolution the timber was cut for shipbuilding and for fuel: iron furnaces like the one we visited at Bonawe swallowed up massive acreages of trees. Naturalists view the replanting programmes with some scepticism. W. R. Mitchell points out that pines, with the exception of Scots pines, are exotic, not native, and lack the bacteria needed to break down their debris. On the other hand, the new forests provide a sheltered habitat for many species of wildlife, some of which – the pine marten for example – were in danger of becoming extinct.

INVEREWE: HORTICULTURAL FEAST

Planting Scots and Corsican pines was the initial step to civilising Am Ploc Ard, a fifty-acre peninsula on Loch Ewe. Fifteen years later in 1880 the windbreak was sufficiently established to introduce eucalyptus and rhododendrons, followed by more exotic species. Today Osgood Mackenzie's world-famous gardens at Inverewe are managed by the National Trust for Scotland and attract a hundred thousand visitors annually. On the same latitude as Cape Farewell in Greenland, Himalayan lilies, Flame flowers from Chile and hydrangeas from Japan flourish in the warmth brought by the Gulf Stream.

One cannot quite describe Osgood Mackenzie as a naturalist. He was given his first gun at the age of nine, and for the next seventy years enjoyed fully the trigger-happy life of the Highland laird. A typical day seems to have gone like this: up at 5.00 am and down to the burn to guddle a couple of fifteen-pound salmon for breakfast. On the way back, picked off a couple of pine martens, a wild cat and a heron. After breakfast, up on the moors for a grouse shoot. Tally: fifteen brace – plus a snow goose and a wild swan. After lunch, a hare shoot with some friends. Had to stop after fifty because the gun got too hot to hold. In the evening, down to the lochan. Only a dozen medium-sized trout, but saw a family of otters and picked them off with the single-bore. Homeward-bound, saw an osprey and . . . you can read about this and about the creation of his gardens in his memoirs, *A Hundred Years in the Highlands*.

Skirting Gruinard Bay we have a fine view of Gruinard Island where the anthrax virus was used in early research into bacteriological warfare. We turn inland to follow the Dundonnell River past the spectacular Ardessie Falls. From Dundonnell village a road of sorts leads to a gourmet's paradise, the Aultnaharrie Inn. If you don't like the look of the road, the hotel has a launch and will transfer diners across Loch Broom from Ullapool.

FILTHY HOLLOW

From Braemore, just after we rejoin the A835, a path leads to Corrieshalloch, 'Filthy Hollow'. 'I think even the most hardened sightseer would pause aghast,' writes G. Douglas Bolton, describing the Falls of Measach from a bridge across the chasm, 230 feet above the water. The suspension bridge, built by Sir John Fowler (later of Forth Bridge fame) when he bought Braemore estate in 1867, is inspected carefully every year. The walls of the gorge are not: leave the path at your peril. The poor light and high humidity of Corrieshalloch create a special habitat. Rare plants and ferns flourish. The roar of the cascade seems to echo in your ears long after you have moved on.

'A beauty of colouring which I have not seen excelled by the Mediterranean' is how Bolton described Loch Broom on a sunny day. (He also compared it, in winter, to an Icelandic fjord.) At its head is Ullapool, built 200 years ago by the British Fisheries Society. The town has changed little over the years. It still has a fishing fleet, though today most of its catch is sold at sea to 'Klondykers' (Eastern-bloc factory ships which can buy, but not catch fish in EC waters), for pelagic processing. MacBrayne's run a ferry from Ullapool to the Outer Hebrides while, closer at hand, a trip to the Summer Isles is a popular excursion.

Ullapool is the end of our route but the intrepid motorist will continue north-west through the most desolate corner of mainland Britain. Skirting Cape Wrath, where 8000 acres constitute the only ship-to-shore shelling range in Europe, you can make your way across to John o' Groats and come back south on the A9.

20

EDINBURGH

*Observe, little girls, the Castle. It is built on a
rock, a volcanic plug. It was from one of these
windows that Mary, Queen of Scots lowered
her baby in a basket, a hundred and eighty-
seven feet down in a high wind.*

Written in the 1930s, Muriel Stark's *The Prime of
Miss Jean Brodie* is a lesson in the middle-class
gentility which has shaped modern Edinburgh. A
hundred years ago the city was run exclusively by Tory
lawyers, which helps explain why the more perceptive
contemporary critics describe it as a film set and a
smug town resting on its laurels. This will not bother
the transient tourist too much. Visitors find it a
beautiful city, which is undeniable. It is a treasure-
house of Georgian and Regency architecture. Visitors
to the International Festival in August find it an
exciting city. They would be less impressed if they
came on a wet weekend in February. A few months
after car-stickers appeared with 'Glasgow: Miles
Better', the city of Hume, Boswell and Stevenson
(and the Aids capital of Europe) responded with
'Edinburgh: Slightly Superior'.

Our classic route round Edinburgh will be

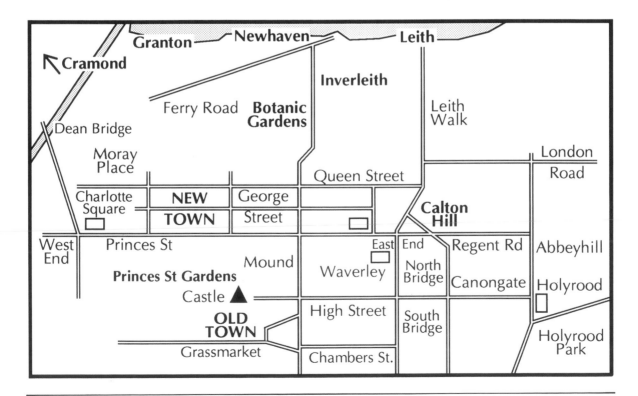

mostly on foot because in summer, in both Old and New Towns, parking spaces are a declining species. Our first section is the Royal Mile, where the patter of visitors' feet and the clicking of cameras are at their loudest. We start at the Castle, whose sprawling mass of grey stone gives 'Auld Reekie' her distinctive skyline.

CASTLE AND ENVIRONS

Scotland's most-visited tourist attraction is well documented in the guide books. It lacks the atmosphere of, say, Craigievar or Blackness but on a clear day there is a great panorama from the ramparts: the Pentland Hills to the south, the Forth Bridges to the west, Fife and the Forth estuary to the north, Princes Street and the New Town below. The famous Tattoo is held on the castle esplanade every August. That the seats are sold out well in advance for the twenty performances suggests military parades are still popular, despite the incongruity of their location within an arts festival. Perhaps forty years ago in the shadow of war there may have been a place for a pompous military *son-et-lumière*; today it seems as anachronistic as the procession of tanks in Red Square. The highlight of 1990 was the community singing of wartime songs – *White Cliffs of Dover* and the like. Public thirst for nostalgia is clearly unquenchable.

A few yards downhill the Scotch Whisky Heritage Centre has recently opened to provide visitors with a potted history of the national drink. You ride past tableaux in an electric cart made of whisky barrels while 'peatsmoke' tickles your nostrils. The presentation inclines to romanticism. A lifesize figure of Burns reads some lines about the 'barley bree', a fondness for which contributed in no small measure to the poet's early death. The Centre is not uninteresting, but a visit to a working distillery is better value.

Across the road in the Outlook Tower, the Camera Obscura is a Victorian periscopic device which projects a moving image of the city on to a tabletop by means of lenses and mirrors. An exhibition of early cameras complements the show. The Tower, and many other buildings in the Mile, are a testament to Sir Patrick Geddes (1854–1932), a pioneer of architectural conservation.

Castlehill now opens into the Lawnmarket. Note the first of many 'closes' on the left: the narrow vennels provide rear access to the tenement houses all down the Mile, and often pedestrian short cuts. A short walk through Lady Stair's Close, for example, passes through a courtyard central to tenements and out on to the Mound, with a fine view of Princes Street and the pretentious neo-classical National Gallery and Royal Scottish Academy. These buildings, which contain the cream of Scotland's art collection, are the work of William Playfair.

DOWN THE STEPS

Now we make a slight detour. (We shall return to the Mile fifty yards on, where the Lawnmarket crosses George IV Bridge and becomes the High Street.) Where Johnston Terrace joins the Lawnmarket we turn right down a flight of steps to Victoria Street. Here are smart little shops: some, new boutiques; some, long-surviving Edinburgh institutions like the brushmaker. The Bow Bar is one of the city's best 'howffs'. Apart from a range of unusual whiskies it has, by Scottish standards, a wide choice of real ale. ('Heavy' is the staple Scottish pint. Drink lager at your peril – it may mean 'store' in German, but in Britain it spells Large and Greedily Excessive Remuneration.) Keeping left past the Traverse Theatre, notable for experimental drama, we cross the east end of the Grassmarket. A generation ago it was a slum and red-light district but it is now cleaned up. In medieval times it was the town boundary: south of here was nothing but pasture and grazing.

The Cowgate leads out of the Grassmarket. It would take us shortly to St Cecilia's Hall, where tourists and locals alike have yet to discover the remarkable Russell Collection of early keyboard instruments, but we turn right up the short steep Candlemaker Row. The canine statue at the top is one of the capital's famous landmarks. Greyfriars Bobby was the hero of an apocryphal story of the fidelity of man's best friend: for fourteen years he guarded his shepherd master's grave in nearby Greyfriars churchyard. Opposite, Chambers Street runs east past the Royal Museum of Scotland, where generations of Edinburgh schoolchildren have flocked to the working machinery in the industrial section, for years before the term 'hands-on' was coined. The building's interior is considered one of the most elegant examples of structural cast iron to survive from Victorian times.

This is the university quarter. The college buildings are scattered over some acres to the south and south-east. Edinburgh is not the oldest university in Scotland – that distinction belongs to St Andrews – but it is the largest, and a novel feature is the Department of Parapsychology, founded in 1983 from a bequest by Arthur Koestler. We turn left along George IV Bridge, passing between Edinburgh City Library and the National Library of Scotland, past the unimaginative Lothian Regional Council headquarters, and turn right into the High Street at Deacon Brodie's Bar.

Inspiration for Stevenson's *Jekyll and Hyde*, Deacon Brodie and Burke and Hare were among Edinburgh's notorious citizens. Popular legend portrays them as body-snatchers. In reality, Burke and Hare kept a lodging-house where they plied their guests with drink and suffocated them while they slept, selling their bodies to the anatomist Robert Knox. Brodie provided the respectable façade. The enterprise was not to last. All came to sticky ends, one of them ending up, with poetic justice, on the dissecting table.

HEART OF EDINBURGH

St Giles church is often referred to as a cathedral. It is the High Kirk of Edinburgh and was completed in 1558, just in time to witness the Reformation. From its pulpit John Knox preached against Mary, Queen of Scots and her 'monstrous regimen [government] of women'. Outside in Parliament Square is the 'Heart of Midlothian', cobbles set into the pavement marking the site of the city's first jail. The Edinburghers' insanitary habit of spitting in it for luck is nowadays confined to elderly people.

Buildings steeped in history, a dozen edifices restored as museums, kiltmakers, sandwich bars and pubs, boutiques and gift shops full of tartan tat . . . the Royal Mile today is a street, or rather four successive streets, of contrast. In summer you can hardly move for tourists and buskers. Then,

ADVOCATES' CLOSE: one of the many alleyways off Edinburgh's High Street where bodysnatchers used to prowl.

LADY STAIR'S CLOSE: attractive pedestrian shortcut from the Lawnmarket to the Mound.

CITY SKYLINE FROM HOLYROOD PARK: the Grecian monument is 'Edinburgh's Disgrace', fortunately unfinished.

surprisingly, you come across a butcher's or a paper shop. Ordinary people still live here after all. The Mile has not yet become the longest open-air museum in the world.

Anchor Close, where the first edition of the *Encylopaedia Britannica* was published – opposite is the Festival Fringe Society and further down the street is the Museum of Childhood, a long-established collection of Victorian and Edwardian toys – directly opposite is Chalmers Close, down which is the excellent Brass Rubbing Centre – John Knox's House (you've guessed it, a museum) – St Mary's Street, where Boswell and Johnson lodged – The People's Story, a new museum – Huntly House, an old one (sixteenth-century plaques on its walls reply in Latin to criticisms of the architecture and when this so-called 'Speaking House' was restored in 1932 a new one was added: *Antiqua tamen Juvenesco*, 'I am old but growing younger') – Queensberry House, former home of the 2nd Duke of Queensberry, ostracised for accepting a £12,000 bribe to sign the Treaty of Union – Moray House, where that Treaty was signed in 1707 . . . It is almost a relief to reach Holyrood at the end of the Mile.

ROYAL RESIDENCE

Holyrood Abbey was founded by David I around 1198 for his Augustinian monks. The Palace was added in the 'Golden Age' of James IV following his marriage to Princess Margaret Tudor of England in 1503, a union of the thistle and the rose. It is visitable today when the Royal Family are not in residence (normally July). Besides relics of Mary, Queen of Scots, the Palace has a hundred and one portraits of the Scottish monarchy, all painted by the same hand, all looking remarkably alike and most of them historically bogus.

In the Palace Yard, note the fountain designed by Robert Matheson. The figures which decorate it are the work of Charles Doyle (father of Sir Arthur Conan), who died obscurely in a city asylum a hundred years ago.

Behind the Palace in Holyrood Park is another extinct volcano, Arthur's Seat. You can drive round the perimeter on the Radical Road; a popular outing for Edinburghers includes feeding the ducks and

swans on the three lakes. You can also drive to within 200 feet of the summit and take a short walk to another of the city's fine viewpoints.

EDINBURGH'S DISGRACE

From Holyrood we go left up Abbeyhill and left into Regent Road. This wide sweep into the heart of the east end offers panoramic views over Holyrood and the Park. The Greek temple lookalike on the right is the former Royal High School. The new school is in the suburbs; the original, where Sir Walter Scott was one of many famous pupils, was in the Cowgate.

Above the building is Calton Hill. It is well worth the climb: R. L. Stevenson considered the view from the top the best in Edinburgh, and today's calendar photographers confirm it. The incomplete Parthenon copy on top is called 'Edinburgh's Disgrace'. Started as a monument to the Napoleonic Wars, it got only so far before subscriptions dried up. It was probably just as well: what you see today is about one-twentieth of what is shown on the plans. Before you descend, the Observatory is worth a closer look. The new building incorporates the Old Observatory, the only surviving building by James Craig, architect of Edinburgh's New Town. (He laid out the street plan but the individual buildings were designed by speculators.)

The biggest architectural disaster since Stevenson's day is the St James Centre, opposite us on Princes Street where we turn right into Leith Street. Film directors looking for a concrete jungle set need look no farther, inside or out. Just behind it is Old Register House, where you might begin to trace your Scottish ancestors. Close by, in a narrow street, is the Café Royal, one of Edinburgh's oldest pubs, where the nineteenth-century *literati* met for oysters and conversation. The Victorian decor, murals and stained glass are still in place. In front of Old Register House is Sir John Steell's equestrian statue of Wellington. The quip at the time was 'the Iron Duke in bronze by Steell'.

We've seen the Royal Mile. Leith Street and Leith Walk are a retail mile. Ironmongers, second-hand electrical shops, Asian grocers, Italian delicatessens . . . this wide historic thoroughfare, once the main exit from Edinburgh to the south, has an air of seediness but a line of trees planted down the middle will one day give it a Continental aspect.

ON THE WATERFRONT

Years ago respectable people did not go to Leith after dark. Like ports all round the world, it was a red-light district and had a reputation for violent crime. As to its river, there used to be seventy mills along twenty miles of the Water of Leith and Edinburgh's sewage joined the effluent pouring into Leith docks.

The gentrification of Leith began ten years ago when a brave entrepreneur opened a restaurant. Wine bars followed and the yuppies moved in. Today there is a wild diversity of architecture and atmosphere. Here is a row of nineteenth-century merchants' houses, long since converted into flats. There is a street of expensive renovations. Round the corner is a grim grey barracks with barred windows, which you might mistake for a prison. Actually it is a bonded-whisky warehouse. Opposite is a floating restaurant: *African Queen*, *Ocean Mist*, *Ocean Breeze* . . . the name changes about once a week and bar prices are as inventive as the ambience. Two streets uptown, a four-storey psychedelic mural covers the gable-end of a tenement. Some Social Work Director's solution to the problem of graffiti? It underlines how lacking Edinburgh is in frivolity.

The tourists make for Lamb's House, oldest in Leith, where Mary, Queen of Scots stayed. We make for Crabbies, for a unique factory tour of their Green Ginger Winery. The wine, made not only from ginger but also from sultanas, citrus peel and spices, is the other ingredient in that popular cold-weather cocktail, the Whisky Mac. The situation is appropriate for in their prime the docks were stacked high with exotic spices and fruits.

Leith, port of commerce, is flanked by other ports which also were once separate villages. Going west, Newhaven was a fishing harbour. Farther back it was the headquarters of James IV's Scottish Navy. Granton is now a yacht marina; in former times a ferry crossed to Burntisland in Fife. (The journey is described in A. J. Cronin's *Hatter's Castle*, the first stage of the hero's fatal trip.) Between Granton and Newhaven are two more celebrated hostelries, the Old Chain Pier and the Starbank. The ordinary

visitor doesn't venture west of Granton Square: Pilton and Muirhouse are the city's combat zones.

Instead we go south to Ferry Road and on to Inverleith Row. The entrance to the Royal Botanic Gardens is on the right.

A welcome oasis of colour and shade when the city streets are packed, the Gardens have the largest rhododendron collection in the world. Two classic Victorian hothouses tower over their spiky modern equivalents. They are stuffed with rare orchids, exotic palms, banana trees and giant water-lilies. Inverleith House (previously the Gallery of Modern Art) in the middle of the site belongs to the Royal Botanic Gardens and houses botanically-related exhibitions from time to time. The Gallery of Modern Art moved to a former school building off Belford Road and after considerable renovation was formally reopened in 1986.

THE GEORGIAN CITY

An inconspicuous plaque marks the house on Inverleith Row where Robert Louis Stevenson was born, just before we cross the Water of Leith in front of the Canonmills clock. We turn right and begin a long climb which culminates in the heart of the New Town. With the Royal Scottish Academy in front, we are in the centre of a grid-iron pattern, the brainchild of George Drummond, five times Lord Provost of Edinburgh. Going west along George Street through the city's financial sector we come to Charlotte Square. Designed by Robert Adam in the last year of his life, it is considered the most triumphant of his urban schemes. The north side is the oldest and best preserved. The National Trust for Scotland has its offices at No. 5 and its showpiece 'Georgian House' at No. 7. Number 6 is the official residence of the Secretary of State for Scotland. In Victorian times Charlotte Square was Edinburgh's Harley Street; among other pioneers of medicine, Joseph Lister lived here.

Some find the geometry of this area monotonous, all squares and straight lines. But a street or two north are the circuses and curved terraces of the northern New Town, designed by James Graham for the Earl of Moray. Moray Place, a twelve-sided circus, is the centrepiece of this area between the New Town and the Water of Leith.

PRINCES STREET: famous view of a famous street, from Calton Hill.

ROYAL BOTANIC GARDENS, EDINBURGH: spiky modern glasshouses and their graceful Victorian counterparts are stuffed with exotic plants.

LEITH: Edinburgh's port; within living memory a slum and red-light district, now home to upmarket wine bars.

WEST END TO EAST END

From Charlotte Square the short arm of the 'J' that is Queensferry Street leads into the West End of Princes Street. The famous street, Scotland's most prestigious address for a shop, is a cheerful mixture of architectural styles. Since the early nineteenth century, bitter legal battles have kept the south side shopless, giving Princes Street what estate agents call an open aspect. On the north side, fast-food outlets and department stores have replaced all the old cherished family businesses except Jenners, the Harrods of Edinburgh. Even with the recent introduction of escalators, it is easy to get lost in Jenners' labyrinthine interior.

Opposite stands the Scott Monument, built in 1844. The elaborate Gothic tower, like the spire of a truncated cathedral, is the creation of George Kemp, self-taught architect whose design won an open competition. Inside the wedding-cake tiers are 287 steps taking you to a viewpoint 200 feet above Princes Street.

There are three unusual clocks in Princes Street. The first projects from the wall of a department store at the West End. Try to catch this supreme example of kitsch on the hour: a line of kilted Highlanders proceeds around the base while the chimes strike. The second clock is in Princes Street Gardens, which were formed when the Nor' Loch dividing Old and New Towns was drained in the 1760s. This was the world's first floral clock, laid out in 1903.

Don't set your watch by the third clock, above the Balmoral Hotel at the East End. By old Edinburgh custom it is kept a few minutes fast to encourage travellers to get to their trains on time.

In the shadow of the Balmoral is the subterranean Waverley Market, a high-tech complex of specialty shops in an area of ponds, fountains and glass-walled lifts. From the flat roof, where an attempt has been made to create a piazza, there is access to the city's tourist information services. In bookshops and on bookstalls you can pick up a copy of *The List*, an estimable publication with news and reviews of what's on in both Edinburgh and Glasgow.

Our classic route ends at Waverley station – as any Glaswegian will tell you, the finest thing to come out of Edinburgh is the train to Glasgow, and that's where we're Glasgowing next. Our quick circuit has missed out some of the capital's major attractions: the only breeding penguin colony outside Antarctica, at the Edinburgh Zoo in Corstorphine (*Croix d'Or Fine?*); the deco frontage of the Maybury roadhouse, past Corstorphine on the edge of the city; Macsweens of Bruntsfield, who export haggis all over the world; Marchmont, where there was once a girls' school called St Trinnean's (*sic*), immortalised by cartoonist Ronald Searle; Merchiston Tower, former home of John Napier, deadly enemy of schoolchildren down the ages for inventing logarithms and the digital calculator; and Cramond on the Forth. It was to Cramond, known to the Romans and now a tiny yachting centre, that Miss Jean Brodie brought her girls, her *'crème de la crème'*, on Sunday afternoons; an excursion enjoyed by many Edinburghers at the present day.

21

GLASGOW

When in Scotland you probably carry pieces of Glasgow's history in your pocket. On the reverse of a Bank of Scotland note is the picture of a sailing ship, the logo of Glasgow's first bank. The Ship Bank of 1750, now demolished, stood at the corner of the Saltmarket and Bridgegait, two of the original eight streets of the city. David Dale of New Lanark, whom we met at the beginning of this book,

was the agent of the first Glasgow branch of the Royal Bank.

The ship is an apt symbol for Glasgow since the city's wealth, like that of Liverpool, came initially from foreign trade. There is clear evidence of this today: the streets which grew from the old town carry the names of the tobacco barons and the countries they traded with.

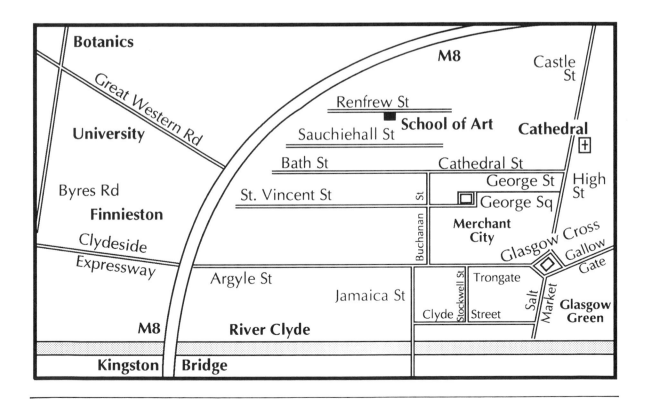

TEMPLETON'S CARPET FACTORY, GLASGOW: famous landmark off Glasgow Green, a copy of the Doge's Palace in Venice.

ST ANDREW'S CHURCH: off the Clyde Walkway, reflected in its surprising annexe.

The symbols on Glasgow's coat-of-arms are much older. They relate to legends associated with St Mungo, who in AD 543 came to set up his monastic cell on the banks of the Molendinar Burn, where the cathedral stands today. At the same time a community of salmon fishers had settled half a mile downstream, where the Molendinar flowed into the Clyde. The famous story about Mungo, which has counterparts in legends across the world, concerns King Rydderch and his beautiful wife Languoreth. Attracted to a handsome young courtier, the Queen injudiciously gave him a ring, a present from her husband. The King noticed the ring and, in a rest period during a royal hunt, pulled it off the sleeping courtier's finger and threw it into the Clyde; then

ordered Languoreth to produce it. She ran in a panic to St Mungo, who advised her to send a messenger to fish in the Clyde. He landed a salmon with the ring in its mouth, marital harmony was restored and the fish and ring are prominent on the city's shield.

GREEN PLACE OR GREY DOG?

Experts disagree about the derivation of Glasgow's name. *Glas* can mean green, grey or stream; *ghu* could be dear, rock or dog. You can therefore take your pick between the several combinations of the words, from 'dear green place' to 'grey dog' – 'greyhound' was Mungo's nickname. For about twelve centuries after the saint's time, Glasgow

GEORGE SQUARE, GLASGOW: Sir Walter Scott towers above a dozen statues of the famous.

GEORGE SQUARE: lions guard Glasgow's City Chambers, built during the city's industrial zenith.

appears to have been a peaceful settlement. Unlike Edinburgh and Stirling, the town was never fortified. The 'gaits' referred to on old maps are merely 'ways to' – Trongait being the 'way to the Tron'.

When Bonnie Prince Charlie, mean-mooded in retreat, arrived to sack the city, the inhabitants quickly raised £10,000 to feed and reclothe his army. A couple of hundred years earlier during the Reformation, members of the Incorporated Trades of Glasgow threw a cordon round the cathedral. A deal was struck and the Reformers were allowed in to destroy any Catholic relics provided they left the fabric of the building intact. As a consequence, Glasgow Cathedral is the best-preserved building of its type on the Scottish mainland.

Twenty years before the Jacobites, Daniel Defoe was in Scotland, a government spy thinly disguised as a writer. He wrote of Glasgow: 'It is a large, stately and well-built city . . . one of the cleanliest, most beautiful in Britain.'

The city was then enjoying the benefits of trade: rum and sugar from Jamaica, tobacco from Virginia. (History usually casts a discreet veil over a nice little spin-off for the tobacco barons. Outward bound, their ships made a detour via the coast of Africa to take on cargoes of slaves.)

Those halcyon days came to an end with the American War of Independence. By the year 1800 Glasgow was in a social and environmental nose-dive which would last for 150 years.

NO MEAN CITY

And through my heart, as through a dream,
Flows on that Black disdainful stream

When Alex Smith described the Clyde, Glasgow was the boiler-house of the Industrial Revolution. In the 1760s a young engineer called James Watt had walked on Glasgow Green sketching out his plans for steam propulsion and by 1850 the city had become the workshop of the Empire. In fifty years the population increased from 77,000 to 329,000 as immigrant Irish, casualties of the 'Hungry Forties', and Highlanders, victims of the Clearances, arrived in droves to look for work in the shipbuilding and locomotive industries. In the second half of the century the population doubled and speculative builders responded by cramming it into shoddy tenements. Some, built as slums, survived as slums well into the 1950s.

In 1934 the *News of the World* noted that 'it is not uncommon for eight, ten or twelve people to be herded together in a single room . . . there are 175,000 "houses" without baths'. This was the era powerfully described in Alexander McArthur's *No Mean City* – the infamous Gorbals, deprivation and squalor, razor gangs, oblivion attained with 'red biddy', a cocktail of cheap wine and methylated spirit bought in a shebeen or illegal drinking den. Even the Second World War made little impact on slum lifestyles: reformed murderer Jimmy Boyle and Tom McGrath's play, *The Hard Man*, published in the 1970s, paints much the same picture as McArthur's study.

SIX MILES BETTER

Sceptics pointed out that when the inner-city slums were eventually demolished their inhabitants were merely transferred to outer-city slums like Easterhouse and Drumchapel. But on the streets of Glasgow today there is a buoyancy and an optimism which would have been unthinkable a generation ago. Future historians will probably ascribe the restoration of civic pride to three recent events: the opening of the Burrell Collection, the 1983 Museum of the Year; the 1988 Garden Festival; and the city's nomination as Culture Capital of Europe in 1990.

Our classic route through Glasgow is from east to west and from old to new. We start on Glasgow Green, the oldest public park in Britain and most central of about seventy parks within the city's boundaries. The monument to Lord Nelson recalls an anecdote, to appreciate which you have to know that the Glasgow suburb of Neilston is locally pronounced 'Nelson'.

City councillors are looking at the newly-erected memorial and trying to agree on an inscription. 'Let's keep it simple,' says one. 'How about "TO NELSON"?' – 'Aye,' says another, '"'Tae Nelson, six mile"'. Then we'll hae a milestone as well as a monument.'

Over the centuries the role of the Green has changed. On what was always a popular stamping-ground for orators, the 1848 Chartist riots started with speeches, followed nearly a century later by the soap-box Communists of 'Red Clydeside'. Venue for parades and demonstrations, site of the Glasgow Fair (established by royal charter in 1189) and more recently of open-air rock concerts, the city's best-loved open space may, if the developers' latest dreams come true, lose a third of its area to a Disneyland.

PALACE OF VARIETIES

The Green's public buildings, People's Palace and Winter Garden, were built in 1898 with compensation from the Caledonian Railway Company, which wanted to run a railway underneath. Community museums are sometimes accused of being top-heavy with nostalgia, but the collection in the Palace is bizarre enough to impress the most critical eye. The upper floor supports a faithful re-creation of a 'single end', typical housing of the bad old days. Other exhibits range from a prototype steam organ made by James Watt to the 'big banana feet' boots made by playwright John Byrne for Billy Connolly and a punchbowl from the Saracen's Head which before demolition was the oldest hostelry in the city. It was built in 1754 by Robert Tennent, founder of the brewing family, and its patrons included Samuel Johnson, James Boswell, Robert Burns, John Wesley and William Wordsworth.

On the northern fringe of the Green you can hardly miss Templeton's carpet factory. Built by William Leiper in 1899, it is a copy of the Doge's Palace in Venice and in its prime was the biggest producer of carpeting in Europe, supplying transatlantic liners and hotels around the world. This impressive brick building is now internally sub-divided, a home to small businesses.

Before we start following the Clyde westward, a short detour north will bring us to the oldest part of Glasgow. The Saltmarket leads into Glasgow Cross, where you can trace unsuccessful attempts to make the crossroads a circus in the London style. Victorian builders destroyed many of the fine old buildings in the district, but the Tolbooth still sees the people of Glasgow congregate at Hogmanay. If we turn right along the Gallowgate we come to the 'Barras', the hundred-year-old weekend street market. Though it has become over-commercialised in recent years, the lively patter of the traders is still enjoyable entertainment.

LAUREATE OF THE NURSERY

Going up the High Street into Castle Street, observe Provand's Lordship, built in 1471, the oldest house in Glasgow, opposite the cathedral (open to the public).

Visiting St Mungo's Cathedral you are following in the footsteps of Cromwell, Robert Bruce and Edward I. An eternal lamp burns in the saint's tomb. There are many more tombs in the nearby Necropolis, presided over by a scowling statue of John Knox. The cemetery contains every style of architecture, since it was the fashion for rich merchants to have their memorials represent the countries where they made their fortunes. The 'Laureate of the Nursery' is buried here: William Miller, who wrote *Wee Willie Winkie*.

Back at the Green we follow the river west on Clyde Street and then on the attractive Clyde walkway. Just before the Briggait building, a gem of Victorian design and originally the city fishmarket, a narrow lane is the site of Paddy's Market. Once the finest fleamarket this side of Amsterdam, it is in decline, a casualty of the affluent society. St Andrew's church is another building of note, reflected in an adjacent structure of mirrored glass which is not, as

you might suppose, the office of an insurance company but a daring annexe of the church itself. Sit on one of the benches to watch the river roll by and total strangers will come to pass the time of day with you. Such friendliness in Edinburgh would be suspect – usually the prelude to a hard-luck story and a request for a loan. But in Glasgow it is quite natural and part of the legendary *bonhomie*.

LAUDER AND LAUREL

Where Victoria Bridge crosses the river, Stockwell Street runs north. Fifty yards from here one of Glasgow's renowned music-halls used to stand. The Scotia witnessed the first professional performance of Harry Lauder. Later it became the Metropole, where Arthur Jefferson the manager trained his son in stage-management. Young Stanley changed his name to Laurel and ended up as the doleful half of the silent-movie stars, Laurel and Hardy.

As you can see from old posters in the People's Palace, Glasgow has a long tradition of entertain-ment, mostly at the proletarian level. Will Fyffe was a great favourite in the music-hall era and wrote the words to the city's anthem, *I Belong to Glasgow* (he belonged to Dundee). The tradition has continued down to the present with comedy actors like Robbie Coltrane and Billy Connolly. Throughout the 1980s, as in Liverpool during the 1960s, Glasgow was a breeding-ground for rock groups. Internationally famous groups like Wet Wet Wet, Deacon Blue and Hue and Cry learned the ropes in front of Glasgow audiences. At the other end of the scale, Scottish Opera, Scottish Ballet and the Scottish National Orchestra are all based in Glasgow and not, as you might expect, in Edinburgh.

THE SHOPPING CENTRE

Behind St Andrew's church we catch a glimpse of St Enoch's, formerly a railway station and now a futuristic shopping complex, all glass and neon. Turning north into Jamaica Street, admire above the shopfronts some handsome Victorian frontages. (Glasgow is a city you leave with a crick in the neck, for much of its finest architecture is four or six storeys up.) The pedestrianised section of Argyle Street takes

MERCHANT CITY: dilapidated heart of Glasgow, now under serious redevelopment – 'Glasgow is a city we leave with a crick in our necks.'

PRINCES SQUARE: futuristic shopping centre makes clever use of natural lighting and has *art-nouveau* theme.

THE MITCHELL LIBRARY: with more than a million reference books it is said to be the largest reference library in Europe.

GARNETHILL: gable end mural in Glasgow's 'Chinatown'.

GLASGOW SCHOOL OF ART: Charles Rennie Mackintosh's unique creation; a stunning and innovative piece of architecture.

us to St Enoch's. The toylike Jacobean building between the shopping centre and the entrance to the Underground (known to Glaswegians as the Clockwork Orange) is the City Travel Centre.

We now turn north up Buchanan Street, one of the city's most delightful thoroughfares. The policy of pedestrianising main city streets and planting trees and shrubs is clearly a winner. An innocuous and narrow passage on the right leads straight into a culture shock: Princes Square, an enclosed world of glass lifts, escalators, shops and cafés, wrought iron and stained glass.

Back on Buchanan Street we could detour left along St Vincent Street to browse in John Smith's bookshop. Two hundred years ago people were browsing here over the latest edition of Burns's

poems: the bookseller opened his doors in 1751. Another curious building on the corner is affectionately called by Glaswegians the Hat Rack. Cutting through Royal Exchange Square we come to the administrative heart of the city, George Square. Sir Walter Scott towers above a dozen statues which, with the exception of Victoria and Albert, are all of notable Scots and notable Glaswegians.

The imposing façade of the City Chambers dominates the east side of the Square. Except during civic functions it is possible to go inside and see the massive pillars and arches in Aberdeen granite and multicoloured marble from various Italian quarries. Designed by the Paisley architect William Young, the building suggests the confidence of a city at its industrial zenith.

East of George Square there are more fine buildings in the area known as Merchant City. A generation ago this was almost a slum district. It is now the fashionable place to live and, the way things are going, will soon have a greater number of yuppie wine bars than Soho.

THE MACKINTOSH TRAIL

A few blocks north-west is Sauchiehall Street. 'The majority of Glasgow pubs', wrote Hugh McDiarmid, 'are for connoisseurs of the morose.' At the turn of the century Glasgow pubs were so disreputable that no respectable woman and few respectable men would enter one. So the tearoom was born. In Sauchiehall Street (the name means 'willow meadow') Kate Cranston employed the young Charles Rennie Mackintosh to design her Willow Tearoom. Pilgrims on the Mackintosh Trail can climb to the first floor and drink tea in the claustrophobic little room.

Another Mackintosh shrine, a celebrated one, is a block north. He was only twenty-eight when he won the competition to design the Glasgow School of Art and, if you compare it with the classical buildings around George Square, built only fifty years earlier, you appreciate the importance of Mackintosh's achievement. As was his practice, he designed the interior in harmony with the exterior, right down to the last light-fitting.

On the streets of this quarter you will see Oriental faces: this is Garnethill, Glasgow's Chinatown. Undoubtedly the biggest single factor in making Glasgow a really cosmopolitan city has been the wide ethnic mix it has attracted. It says something for the character of the native Glaswegian that racial integration problems of the kind common in London and Birmingham are virtually unknown.

There is a third unmissable attraction for 'Toshie' fans. We navigate our way west across the M8 motorway and past the domed Mitchell Library (with more than a million books it is said to be the largest reference library in Europe) to the university quarter and the genteel residential suburb of Kelvinside. Within the University at two separate sites are the Hunterian Art Gallery and the Hunterian Museum, in the former, upstairs, you can see a reconstruction of the great architect's own house. Nearby, the baroque Kelvingrove Art Gallery holds a collection which varies from the sublime to the ridiculous, from Dali's once-controversial *Christ of St John of the Cross* to 'sculpture' by local boy Eduardo Paolozzi.

BRIGHT LIGHTS OF THE WEST END

Opposite the Art Gallery, Kelvin Hall houses a transport museum with a reconstructed 1938 street, trams and an Underground station, all large as life. Opposite the Botanic Gardens, which contain the Kibble Palace, a vast Victorian glasshouse where Disraeli and Gladstone addressed election meetings, is the top end of Byres Road, the busiest street outside central Glasgow. From its glitzy top to its more mundane bottom in Partick, smart restaurants and fashionable pubs are on the increase.

The city has much more to offer. We haven't visited the Burrell Collection on this short tour – 8000 antiques and *objects d'art* gifted to the city by a shipping tycoon. We haven't seen Rouken Glen and its Butterfly House; or the Tenement House, the NTS's picture of urban life at the turn of the century; or 'Glasgow's Glasgow', a complex of exhibitions, theatres and bars in the vaults underneath Central Station, so new that its future is uncertain.

We shall return to the river at Finnieston Quay, just a mile downstream from the Green where we started, and perhaps celebrate the end of our journey in the 1950s-style black-and-chrome cocktail bar at the top of the Rotunda. We can look across the Clyde to the South Rotunda and the site of the 1988 Garden Festival. We can reflect on the astonishing success of Glasgow's renaissance. The city's motto is 'Let Glasgow Flourish' – and flourishing it is.

It is dusk and, across the city, lights are coming on: floodlights around the Cathedral and George Square, neon lights at the clubs in Merchant City, lights in the tower blocks in Govan. Forty miles east, Edinburghers are retiring behind thick curtains with cups of cocoa. But Glasgow is a city which never sleeps. At this hour there is a perceptible current, a vibration, as thousands of Glaswegians prepare to go out and sample the rich culture which is their birthright. It is, in local parlance, a 'rerr toon'.

INDEX